DEVOTIONS FOR PEOPLE WHO DON'T DO DEVOTIONS

Library of Congress Control Number: 2023935776

#2658
ISBN: 978-0-88028-517-9
© 2023 Forward Movement

Forward Movement
inspire disciples. empower evangelists.

DEVOTIONS FOR PEOPLE WHO DON'T DO DEVOTIONS

Tim Schenck

Forward Movement
Cincinnati, Ohio

To my brother Matt, whose entrepreneurial spirit
and passion for life never ceases to inspire me.

CONTENTS

Introduction ix

Walk It Off 3

Cemetery Wanderings 5

Pass/Fail 7

Skunked! 9

Starstruck 12

Are You #Blessed? 14

Practice What You Preach 17

Insider Language 20

The Power of No 23

Where Are They Now? 26

Garbage Time 29

The Soundtracks of Our Lives 32

Keeping Up Appearances 35

Life is Not a Highlight Reel 38

Blind Spots 41

Subject to Interpretation 44

Salty Language 47

Staying Focused 50

Seeing the Big Picture 53

Navigating Rough Waters 56

Pardon the Interruption 59

WAIT: Why Am I Talking? 62

Dirty Work 65

Drawing it Up 67

Road Trip 70

Shifting Perspectives 73

Leap of Faith.. 76

Creature of Habit.. 79

Buzz Kill... 82

Chance Encounters 85

Fill Dirt 88

Tuning Peg... 91

Angel's Share 94

Golden Repair... 97

Playing Like Betty White... 100

Science Class 102

Celebrity Status.. 105

Life and Death... 108

Doing the Dishes 110

Backup Camera... 113

On the Bench 115

The Big Sort... 118

Now Boarding.. 121

Round and Round 124

Love Your Enemies... 126

Birthday Song.. 129

Imagine the Possibilities 131

Spiritual Wallflowers... 134

Character Actors... 137

Joy to the World.. 140

Acknowledgments.. 143

About the Author 145

About Forward Movement.. 146

INTRODUCTION

I'm not a big fan of devotional books. You know, the kind you get for Christmas from your Aunt Thelma, whose big smile always comes with a side of judgment. With titles like *Devotions for Dads* or *365 Daily Devotions to Strengthen Your Marriage*, she's not-so-subtly trying to fix what she thinks is wrong with you by jamming religious books into your stocking.

Maybe it's the saccharine sweet, holier-than-thou tone of most of the devotionals I've browsed in the Religion & Spirituality section at Barnes & Noble. Okay, most of those were put out by Joel Osteen, Inc. But still, there's a Ned Flanders-esque vibe to many spiritual books that leaves you wondering if the people who write them even inhabit the same planet. And surely that's not helpful for those of us seeking the divine presence in the midst of our daily lives.

So, here are a few things you should know about this little book. First, there are not 365 devotions. Frankly, I'm just not that prolific. But mostly, I don't want this book to become a source of spiritual guilt, staring at you from your nightstand, begging you to read 12 straight devotions in a single day just to catch up.

Rather, I hope you take as much time with each devotion as you like. That may be 30 seconds, or it may be a week. If the words resonate, lean into them. If they don't, turn the page and keep moving. These are meant to be starting points, not megaphone-style declarations of certainty. The hope is that you will bring your own experience and imagination to these brief reflections and that, through engagement with them, they will offer some inspiration and perspective.

You can certainly read these through a profound theological lens, but that's not really the point. I've tried to simply offer small morsels of real life to be chewed upon. Some will be more flavorful for you than others—those are the ones to spend time with and savor.

Following each devotion, you'll find a brief section called *Reflect & Engage.* You can think about these questions on your own, perhaps with your morning coffee or afternoon tea. Better yet, find a small group of friends or fellow seekers and use these prompts as jumping-off points to get to know one another—and God—in deeper ways. I've found that following a global pandemic, many people want to gather to talk about their lives in the context of faith. Here is an accessible, non-threatening way to do just that.

I firmly believe that God is often most present just beneath the surface of the visible world. If we have eyes to see the divine hand at work in the day-to-day interactions and experiences of our lives, in both the mundane and the miraculous, our lives will be forever enriched. I pray our journey together will help you see things that so often remain unseen. And, in so doing, perhaps this process will help you to unlock your own unique ability to glimpse God in your daily life.

I look forward to spending a bit of time with you throughout these pages. And perhaps we'll even have some fun meeting Jesus along the way.

DEVOTIONS FOR PEOPLE WHO DON'T DO DEVOTIONS

WALK IT OFF

My grace is sufficient for you, for my power is made perfect in weakness. —**2 Corinthians 12:9**

"Walk it off." That was Coach Spencer's answer to everything. Hit in the face with a dodgeball thrown by the biggest bully in school? "Walk it off." Dying of thirst with a touch of heatstroke after the forced one-mile sprint around the perimeter of the campus? "Walk it off."

Coach Spencer's primary role was varsity football coach. This was an exalted position at my school, and a certain aura surrounded Coach Spencer wherever he went. His "other duties as assigned" included overseeing a few sections of middle school gym class, and he clearly believed this was beneath him. That may be why he tortured us with various obstacle courses, cutting us spoiled brats down to size while keeping his eyes peeled for the next star running back.

One day, I tripped and banged my head on the concrete floor during one of his sadistic exercise routines, hard enough that I literally saw stars. The first thing I remember was Coach Spencer standing over me, muttering, "Walk it off, walk it off."

We often take Coach Spencer's approach to life's challenges: we try to "walk it off." We get knocked down, and then we get back up and keep going. And there are absolutely times to demonstrate such resilience: minor setbacks, disappointments, and the various challenges that life sends our way. We're told that nobody wants to hear about our problems, so we suck it up.

But sometimes, we can't just "walk it off." When it comes to our mental and spiritual health, it's okay to let others know when we're struggling. Reaching out to a friend or therapist is not an admission of defeat but strength.

Jesus reminds us that his "power is made perfect in weakness." It's okay to let Jesus do the walking for us while we rest awhile, to allow his grace to carry us. The good news is that Jesus is often most fully present during those times when we feel completely and utterly overwhelmed. The trick is to allow him to walk with us as a true companion along the journey.

Reflect & Engage

Name a time when you couldn't face something alone—a spiritual, emotional, or physical challenge. Did you reach out for help? In retrospect, what might you have done differently?

CEMETERY WANDERINGS

The grass withers, the flower fades; but the word of our God endures forever. —Isaiah 40:8

One of the things I like to do when things are feeling particularly uncertain in the world or I'm just feeling out of sorts in my life is to walk through the historic cemetery down the street.

I know that for some, there is no more depressing place than a cemetery. There's a reason I used to hold my breath whenever I'd drive past one as a kid. In a cemetery, you are literally surrounded by death, and with each gravestone, you come face-to-face with the fleeting nature of life.

But I find that walking through a cemetery is good for the soul. Rather than ghoulish or gloomy, I experience it as a place to reflect on life and faith. A cemetery offers perspective and reminds us that our own troubles, whether personal or professional, placed in the broad context of human history are neither unique nor important.

As I stroll among the headstones, I always return to the prophet Isaiah's verse at the beginning of this devotion. Everything we see, like the grass or the flowers, does indeed pass away, along with our mortal bodies, no matter how much care and attention we've given them over the years.

And our earthly concerns, no matter how seemingly urgent, are of little account in the grand scheme of things. What remains is the eternal nature of God. In these headstones, rather than death, I see hope.

It's helpful to recognize that hope does not come without grief or burden. It is not untouched by pain and brokenness; it is not cut off from sadness or despair. Rather, hope is the light that shines in the darkness. So that whatever we're facing, whatever we're struggling with, whatever difficult situation we're confronting, our hope in the eternal abides.

These are some of my fleeting thoughts as I wander past the seventeenth-century town mothers and fathers in one section and a couple of governors in another and pause to say a quiet prayer at the graves of those parishioners I've buried on this hallowed ground.

⇨ ⇨ ⇨

Reflect & Engage

When was the last time you visited a cemetery? Was it just for a stroll or were you visiting someone in particular? In what ways does wandering through the tombstones of those who have come before you shift your perspective on life?

PASS/FAIL

Do not judge, so that you may not be judged.
—**Matthew 7:1**

The single, ubiquitously American rite of passage must be the driver's license road test. Pass, and you receive a ticket to freedom that accompanies your invitation to the open road. Fail, and you suffer the shame and indignity of being subjected once again to the diabolical whims of the Department of Motor Vehicles.

Everybody remembers their driver's test no matter how many years have passed. Some recall the euphoria of miraculously nailing the dreaded parallel parking portion of the exam. For others, the tester's disappointed face is forever seared into their memory, and they can still viscerally feel the bump of the curb that signaled failure.

Regardless of the outcome, everyone I know shares a memory of profound anxiety in the moments before meeting the evaluator and taking the test. Few times in life are you so intimately and irrevocably judged by another human being. Sure, there are tests in school and performance evaluations at work. But toss in the requisite insecurity of your average 16-year-old and add the discomfort of a stranger with a clipboard sitting next to you, and the driver's test is a recipe for existential teenage angst.

A couple of years ago I discovered something interesting: 16-year-olds don't have a monopoly on pre-road test jitters. My brother bought me a long-coveted scooter for my fiftieth birthday, which was amazing! But it meant I had to take a motorcycle road test. So I found myself lined up with a bunch of nervous teenagers.

Fortunately, with the passage of time comes perspective. Moments that once seemed heartrendingly fraught fade into the blur of memories that make up our lives. I recognized that if I failed my first road test in 35 years (I didn't, thanks be to God), I would live to ride another day.

And as we age, we encounter rivers of uncertainty and fear that matter more than whether we'll be able to drive to the local convenience store for an energy drink now or next month after we retake the road test. All we can do is take each day as it comes and recognize that whatever we're dealing with today is enough. Tomorrow is another day.

Reflect & Engage

Do you remember the emotions you experienced when you took your first road test? How did that day go for you? What other moments in your life have felt like the most important thing at the time but actually were not?

SKUNKED!

Bear one another's burdens, and in this way you will fulfill the law of Christ. —**Galatians 6:2**

The unmistakable smell wafted through the kitchen. Having been down this smelly road once before, Bryna and I knew exactly what had transpired. Delilah, our sweet, then nearly 16-year-old lab/husky rescue dog, had been sprayed by a skunk.

We quickly brought her inside and up to our second-floor bathroom with the walk-in shower, held our noses, and Googled the correct ratio of dish soap, baking soda, and hydrogen peroxide. Within moments, I found myself stripped down and lathering up a wet, smelly, traumatized dog.

While Delilah didn't exactly enjoy the process, she tolerated it. Mostly, I think she realized she needed help and couldn't deal with this experience alone. At least, that was my human projection as she stood stoically in the shower, enduring the frantic machinations around her. If the odor was offensive to my nostrils, I can't imagine what it was like for a dog whose sense of smell is at least 100 times more sensitive than mine.

For non-dogs like you and me, admitting we need help is challenging. After all, we're taught to be independent, and self-sufficiency is held up as a grand American virtue. Yet there are times in our lives when we, like Delilah, simply can't do it alone; moments when we need help and must rely on others.

Most of us would much rather *help* others than *accept help* from others. It's hard to admit when we can't get by on our own merits and sheer will. Yet needing and accepting help isn't admitting weakness; it's simply admitting our humanity.

From a faith perspective, awareness of the divine presence reminds us that, in the end, nothing we do or accomplish is done without God's help. This knowledge eliminates the hubris that we're fully in charge of our lives: we can fool ourselves only until we actually need help, at which point the house of cards comes crashing down around us.

At the same time, we also know that regardless of the particular situation we're facing or the seemingly helpless place we find ourselves, God is present with us through it all. And there's both great freedom and immense comfort in this promise.

⇨ ⇨ ⇨

Reflect & Engage

What's an example of a time when you needed physical or emotional support? Did you accept the help gracefully, or did you struggle with the notion of needing assistance? Would you say you're better at giving or receiving help? Why?

STARSTRUCK

When they saw that the star had stopped, they were
overwhelmed with joy. —**Matthew 2:10**

One year when I was a kid, my father took me to Carnegie
Hall for a concert featuring narration by Willie Stargell, the
Pittsburgh Pirates Hall of Fame first baseman. Being in the
music business himself, my dad knew the conductor. So I
went that evening with the promise, or at least the hope, that
I'd get backstage afterward to meet this baseball legend.

I lived for baseball back then. I knew all the stats and all the
players' uniform numbers. Being from Baltimore, I certainly
wasn't a Pirates fan, a team that had beaten the Orioles in
the World Series twice in the 1970s. But still, I was so excited
to meet a true superstar, I even brought one of Stargell's
baseball cards, hoping he might sign it. My brother still
laughs at the memory of me standing before this giant of a
man, staring with wide eyes, haltingly asking "Mr. Stargell"
to please sign an autograph, and then watching me drop the
card, not once but twice. He graciously signed it for me, but
from a dignity standpoint, this was not my finest hour.

The reality is I was starstruck. Meeting a larger-than-life
sports hero got me all twisted up inside. It was exhilarating
and thrilling and nerve-racking—and reduced me to a
tongue-tied little kid. Which, in fairness, I was.

I often think about my encounter with Willie Stargell in the context of the Magi. The three wise men are quite literally starstruck as they follow the Star of Bethlehem. Their journey is driven by a deep yearning to be in the presence of God, which comes to fulfillment upon their arrival at the manger.

In this sense, being starstruck is something to embrace and encourage. Rather than embarrassment and shame, being starstuck brings hope and solace, meaning and wholeness. Sometimes we meet God awkwardly or with hesitation. But God doesn't care about how we present ourselves, only that we do. When we move past the trepidation of being in the presence of holiness, only then can we be fully present to the divine.

Allow yourself to be starstruck and know that what really matters is your response to the deep yearning in your soul.

⇨ ⇨ ⇨

Reflect & Engage

Think about a time you met a celebrity. How did you feel? Did you embarrass yourself? How did you act? How might you capture that same sense of wonder and awe when approaching God?

ARE YOU #BLESSED?

The LORD bless you and keep you; the LORD make his face to shine upon you, and be gracious to you; the LORD lift up his countenance upon you, and give you peace. —**Numbers 6:24-26**

#Blessed. You often see this hashtag on social media. A picture is shared on Facebook of the perfect family on the perfect mountain on the perfect day with the perfect snow. The sun is shining, everyone is smiling, teeth are gleaming, and skis are perfectly waxed. #Blessed. Or you see it on a celebrity's Instagram post as they're sitting in the VIP lounge of an exclusive Miami Beach club sipping a mango martini. #Blessed.

If the word "blessed" means sacred or set apart by God, I'm not sure this is really what we're talking about here. A more authentic representation of what's being conveyed in these posts might be "#Bragging." Or "#Rich." But it's hard to contradict someone who claims to be blessed without sounding like you're simply jealous. It's almost as if those sharing pictures of their precious corgi sitting on the deck of their yacht are using #Blessed to inoculate themselves from criticism. Or perhaps they genuinely believe that this is how God works—that when God truly loves someone, God conveys fancy vacations and mango martinis.

From a theological perspective, luxurious living is not actually the hallmark of blessedness. In the Christian tradition, Jesus subverts the prevailing wisdom of the day: that wealth is a sign of God's blessing while poverty is a sign of God's wrath. That's not how God works, even if that's what some television preachers would have you believe and some Facebook posts imply.

We need look no further than the well-known Beatitudes to see how Jesus flips this whole notion on its head. "Blessed are you who are poor…Blessed are you who are hungry… Blessed are you who weep…Blessed are the meek…Blessed are the persecuted." These don't sound like very Instagram-worthy posts!

And yet Jesus is very clear that these are precisely the ones who are blessed: the powerless and the vulnerable, the oppressed and the marginalized, the ones who, by the world's standards, are the least and the weak, the lost and the lonely.

God resides in the tears of those who weep, in the hunger pangs of those who go without, in the hurt of those who are rejected. If blessing is a sign of God's presence, then these are the people who are truly #Blessed.

We are not blessed because we own a vacation home in Maine or Florida or can jet off to Europe for a long weekend but by the compassion and kindness we show to those on the margins of society. This great reversal offers hope to a hurting world while demonstrating that neither death nor hopelessness get the last word. God does.

⇨ ⇨ ⇨

Reflect & Engage

What do you think when you hear the word "blessed?" or see the social media tag #Blessed? Has your perception of the word changed over the years? Do you consider yourself blessed? In what ways?

PRACTICE WHAT YOU PREACH

*These people draw near with their mouths and honor
me with their lips, while their hearts are far from me.*
—Isaiah 29:13

"Stop yelling!" When a parent yells at a child to stop yelling,
it's the ultimate do-as-I-say-not-as-I-do moment. Every
parent's been there. You're in the car, trying to listen to
the voice on your GPS leading you to an out-of-the-way
apple orchard for some quality family time or you're sitting
in heavy traffic because there's an accident up ahead and
the kids are whining from the back seat because they are
simultaneously "starving" and have to go to the bathroom
even though you just stopped five minutes ago. To top it off,
they're loudly arguing and yelling at each other about who's
on whose side.

"Stop yelling!" The moment those words, hurled in utter
frustration, leave your lips, you're aware of how ridiculous
you sound. Yelling at someone to stop yelling is like telling
someone to give up smoking while chain-smoking unfiltered
Camels. It's just a bit…hypocritical.

You may know that the word "hypocrite" comes from the
world of the theater. In ancient Greece, hypocrite was used
to describe an actor, and it literally meant "one who wears

a mask." Over time, it came to refer to someone wearing a figurative mask. In other words, it meant a person pretending to be someone they're not.

Public examples of hypocrisy, unfortunately, abound: the family-values politician who gets caught up in a prostitution sting; the pastor who preaches about compassion and justice but preys on children; the celebrity who constantly posts on Twitter about the impact of climate change but takes private jets everywhere. The list goes on and on.

But it would be, well, hypocritical, to point out the hypocrisy in others without acknowledging our own hypocrisy. And make no mistake, we are all hypocrites in certain aspects of our lives, whether we're yelling at our children to stop yelling or claiming to be tolerant of others' opinions unless they disagree with us or encouraging people to donate to causes but not actually donating ourselves.

If you are living a life of contradiction, one where your actions are opposed to your values, you can't help but be bound by internal strife and deep shame. And that's not what God wants for any of us. God understands that we are imperfect, complicated, multidimensional beings. That is why we are simply invited to shed as much hypocrisy as humanly possible, both for the sake of our own souls and for those impacted by our actions.

Take stock of your life and look at where hypocrisy may be getting the best of you. And remember, practicing what you preach isn't just for literal preachers.

⇨ ⇨ ⇨

Reflect & Engage

Name some public examples of hypocrisy. How did hearing about them make you feel about the person in question? What are some areas in your own life where you could be better about practicing what you preach?

INSIDER LANGUAGE

Pleasant words are like a honeycomb, sweetness to the soul and health to the body. —**Proverbs 16:24**

"The Danish thing." If you asked anyone outside of my family what this refers to, you'd get a confused look. But within our family, everyone knows exactly what we're talking about: "the Danish thing" is the sleek wooden piece of furniture upon which the TV sits in our family room.

"The Danish thing" has been in my family for years. My parents bought it at a long out-of-business Scandinavian furniture store in Baltimore sometime in the 1970s. Originally it held my father's stereo equipment, prominently featuring his beloved turntable. I inherited it from my mother a few years after he died when my wife and I moved into our first apartment. It's been part of our furniture menagerie ever since, joining us for four interstate moves and the introduction of various children and pets along the way.

I casually referred to it recently in earshot of a visiting friend, who gave me a quizzical look. As I found myself explaining what my seemingly random invocation of a Scandinavian country meant, it occurred to me that every family has its own insider language. Almost every household, for instance, can identify and point out their "junk drawer," that catch-all home to assorted keys, coins, tape, rubber bands, Pokemon cards, half-eaten packages of Skittles, screwdrivers, and phone chargers.

But this is just the tip of the family-specific lexicon iceberg. These include using pet nicknames for one another, calling the family sedan "the old gray mare," having unusual names for specific rooms in the house, or referring to that big mixing bowl used for making chocolate chip cookie batter as "Big Red."

The words and phrases used by families help form a communal identity, creating a tribe-specific vocabulary. As you think about the words of your own family of origin or your current situation, you will likely encounter a mix of practical descriptors and inside jokes.

In the church, we also have insider language, which is a mixed blessing. At one level, calling a cup a "chalice" and a plate a "paten," and calling the entryway the "narthex" adds mystery and heightens the sense that to enter a church is to journey into sacred space. In fact, the word "holy" means "set apart," and this otherworldly language does just that: it sets apart that which we view as God's realm.

But this language can also exclude, and therein lies a danger. The message of divine mercy, compassion, and hope is subverted when the church acts like a club rather than a place of open invitation to all. I love the magical, sacred words of ecclesiastical language, but they must not be used as a way to create insiders and outsiders. There's enough division in this world, and we certainly don't need to add to it.

By the way, "the Danish thing" is looking a bit tired and wobbly these days, and perhaps it's time to send it off to the great furniture store in the sky. But whatever its fate, hearing the phrase always makes me smile.

Reflect & Engage

What are some family-specific words or phrases you use in your household? What memories do these objects evoke for you? Can you think of ways that insider language forms identity while also having the potential to exclude others?

THE POWER OF NO

Let your word be "Yes, Yes" or "No, No;" anything more than this comes from the evil one. —**Matthew 5:37**

"We don't use the word 'no' in our home."

A friend of mine recently told me her teenage daughter is babysitting for a family who made this declaration. Shunning the word "no" is apparently a hot new parenting trend, as mothers and fathers seek a solutions-based approach to child-rearing rather than a punitive model.

So, when a child demands a box of Sugary Sugar Bombs cereal at the grocery store, rather than declare "No!" in a booming, Zeus-like voice, a parent seeks to engage and turn the conversation into a lesson. "I know you'd really like that cereal, but all the sugar wouldn't be good for your teeth. Let's find a healthier option."

Of course, trying to reason with a two-year-old sounds like a recipe for a meltdown, but what do I know? My kids are now Sugary Sugar Bombs-eating young adults. But then, every generation is amazed the previous generation even made it to adulthood, and every generation thinks the previous generation got parenting wrong. It's the circle of parenting life.

Frankly, it's amazing I survived the choking hazards of my playpen. It's amazing my mother and father survived without car seats and seat belts. And evidently, it's amazing my own children survived the constant barrage of hearing "no." "No, you can't have a pet giraffe. No, we can't trade in the minivan for a bulldozer. No, you can't root for the Yankees."

But I worry about children for whom the word "no" is *verboten*. The reality is that life is full of "no," and the sooner you learn to cope with disappointment or find the resilience to circumnavigate it, the better.

When it comes to the life of prayer, it's often said that God offers three responses: yes, no, and wait. You don't necessarily receive these responses as text messages. More often, they are discernible through the unfolding actions and events of your life. It's difficult when the answer is "no," especially when we seek something important to us or to those we love.

But "no" is often the answer, shielding us from situations that would negatively impact our lives or those around us, even if (and especially when) we remain blind to the hidden reasons. That's where this whole faith thing comes in. When the answer is "no," the first impulse may be to stomp our feet and yell at God. Yet even a "no" response means that God is listening and playing an active role in our lives.

At the risk of sounding like someone who, back in my day, walked two miles to school in the snow, without shoes,

uphill both ways, children must hear "no" to learn
hard lessons that will ultimately allow them to thrive.
In the meantime, I have some sugary cereal to eat.

Reflect & Engage

Name a time in your life when the answer to prayer was "no."
How did this turn out for you in the end? Can you think
of some positives that have come out of negative responses
for you?

WHERE ARE THEY NOW?

Do not say, "Why were the former days better than these?" For it is not from wisdom that you ask this.
—Ecclesiastes 7:10

My favorite *Sports Illustrated* issue of the year came in the mail recently. No, not *that* issue. That one comes the week after the Super Bowl, and I'm decidedly not in the market for a new swimsuit.

I'm referring to the magazine's annual "Where Are They Now?" feature. For years, *Sports Illustrated* has devoted a special issue to catching up with stars who long ago left the bright lights of the headlines. Some of these athletes remain in the public consciousness, while others have drifted away as quickly as they burst onto the scene.

This is basically a nostalgia issue, a bone tossed to my generation. When I find the time to sit down with the magazine, there's always a lot of inner "Oh, yeah! I remember that guy. I wonder what he's been up to since his glory days?"

It's hard to know why these stories resonate so deeply. Part of it is voyeurism, to be sure. Who among us *hasn't* Googled an old girlfriend or boyfriend? But mostly, these stories play to the natural longing for connections to our past. If I can learn what a childhood hero of mine has been up to of late, say former Orioles slugger Eddie Murray, I can somehow reconnect to a part of my life. Suddenly, I'm an eight-year-old sitting in the stands with my late father at the since-demolished Memorial Stadium in Baltimore with a 75-cent hot dog in one hand and my baseball glove in the other, chanting "Ed-die, Ed-die!"

These articles often convey a deep sense of humanity. During a star's playing days, we're mostly concerned with statistics and onfield performance. We rarely stop to consider the kind of person we may be rooting for or against. Players have images, but these are often highly crafted by agents and public relations professionals. Here, then, is a glimpse behind the curtain, a chance to see someone outside the lines.

This unvarnished humanity reminds us that these sports stars aren't superheroes but people like you and me, albeit with particular talents and supernatural hand-eye coordination. Or, from a spiritual perspective, they are all children of God, reflecting all the joys and imperfections of humanity. Some have gone on to find new passions—former Red Sox star Kevin Youkilis runs an award-winning brewery in California—and some have encountered more tragedy than acclaim—William "The Refrigerator" Perry battles alcoholism and issues of mental health.

There are lessons for all of us embedded in these stories. We're reminded that life does indeed go on. Some of us remain prisoners of the past; some of us move on to new and exciting challenges. Most of us stay somewhere in-between. But it's important to reflect on our lives, even while looking ahead to the future. We all have various chapters in our lives, though not necessarily ones lived out on highlight reels. And we must continually seek ways to stay in the game.

Reflect & Engage

Which childhood heroes are you most interested in following up on? When did you first realize that celebrity image doesn't always mesh with reality? How have your values or perspective changed since your own "glory days?"

GARBAGE TIME

For everything there is a season, and a time for every matter under heaven. —Ecclesiastes 3:1

Garbage time. In basketball, that's what people call the last few minutes of a blowout. It's the time when the outcome of the contest has already been decided, and the two teams are literally just running out the clock before they head to the showers. Since no coach wants to risk an injury to a star player during the last few meaningless minutes, garbage time is ruled by subs and rookies. It's a time for third-stringers to shine, a chance to make a positive impression on coaches and dazzle fans with hidden prowess. Alas, there's a reason most of these players haven't cracked the starting lineup: they're just not that good.

There are times in our lives when it feels like we're just running out the clock—when we spend more time anticipating future events rather than living in the present: waiting for toddlers to get out of diapers, waiting to receive a coveted promotion, waiting to finally become empty nesters. If we're not careful, we can spend a significant portion of our lives in a self-imposed garbage time. And that's a sad and joyless state in which to exist.

So how do we break out of this? How do we find joy in the present even as we anticipate that which is to come? If I had an easy answer, I would have already written a best-selling self-help book. But I do have a couple of tips. I find that setting aside a few moments each day of intentional, contemplative silence keeps life in perspective and makes me mindful of the small joys that permeate my daily life. Silence forces me to step off the metaphorical treadmill, walk away from my electronic devices, and reflect upon the often taken-for-granted blessings of my life.

Sure, silence can be both elusive and scary. It's difficult to carve out moments of quiet in our fast-paced existence, and silence forces us to confront things about ourselves we might prefer to drown out. Yet it also brings balance to our souls and delight for our small, unheralded triumphs.

In the church year, we often talk about "Ordinary Time." These seasons are not ordinary in the sense of being boring or useless. Rather they are so named because they reflect the fact that, liturgically speaking, they are not dedicated to a particular season or observance.

Some people might see these long periods as the church's garbage time. There's nothing flashy about them. There's no festive Christmas Eve midnight mass or stark service of Good Friday during Ordinary Time. You won't encounter colorful vestments or over-the-top processions. And yet, when it comes to faith, there's no such thing as garbage time.

All time is holy and sanctified and blessed;
no time is meaningless or insignificant or unworthy
of praise. Indeed, the most surprising moments of our
lives often occur when we least expect them.

I encourage you to be aware of areas of your life you may
be treating as garbage time and commit to changing your
approach. The game of life is too short to waste.

Reflect & Engage

Have you experienced periods of "garbage time" in your life?
In what ways have you broken out of them to see God's hand
at work? Where do you find the extraordinary amid the
ordinary?

THE SOUNDTRACKS OF OUR LIVES

Be filled with the Spirit, as you sing psalms and hymns and spiritual songs among yourselves, singing and making melody to the Lord in your hearts.
—**Ephesians 5:18b-19**

Whenever I watch a show on Netflix or see a movie in the theater, I'm always struck by how dramatic the scenes are: the courtroom encounters, the romantic professions of love, the stirring chase scenes. And then, I contrast this with my own life, and the interactions I have on a daily basis feel somehow...lacking.

It finally struck me one day that this feeling is not so much the lack of drama in my life—I mean, I don't engage in many high-speed chases with guns blazing, but I do have some exciting things happen occasionally. What I realized is that what's missing in the drama of my life is an accompanying soundtrack. What makes so many of these TV and movie moments tug at the heartstrings or get the heart pumping is the music that matches the movement.

That training scene in *Rocky* set to "Gonna Fly Now" wouldn't fly if Sylvester Stallone was doing one-armed pushups and punching raw meat set to, say, "The Sound of Silence,"—or simply silence. Can you imagine Darth Vader entering a scene in the *Star Wars* movies without composer John Williams' iconic "Imperial March?" Music sets the mood, heightens the drama, and intensifies the emotions that go with the script.

Sure, there's a bit of emotional manipulation, as when the crescendo builds to the climactic fight scene in a Bruce Lee movie or the classic combination of strings, tuba, and trombone used to create the *Jaws* soundtrack.

We don't have this in our lives, at least not to the same degree. No one plays "Eye of the Tiger" when I stumble into Planet Fitness before work; there's no on-call string section to play soothing background music when I visit a dying parishioner in the hospital; there's no trumpet fanfare when I do the dishes without being asked.

But none of this means our lives are any less dramatic than what we witness on our screens. Less purely entertaining, perhaps; not neatly wrapped up in one-hour chunks, maybe. Yet our lives do play out in high definition, albeit without the accompanying real-time soundtrack.

This begs the question, what *would* your life's soundtrack be? If you're like me, it would likely change depending on your mood and situation, spanning the range of human emotions. There are times when we need encouragement and comfort, inspiration and hope, empowerment and strength.

I'm a big fan of the blues precisely because they encompass a wide range of emotions: joy, grief, anger, hope, faith, love, betrayal, sadness, and possibility. In the next moment, I may listen to the *Magnificat* by sixteenth-century Italian church musician Giovanni Palestrina, a master of Renaissance polyphony. And then I may crank up some AC/DC.

In other words, the soundtrack of my life, like life itself, is complicated. And I imagine, yours is as well. Dramatic, full of contradictions, boring at times, overscheduled at others, messy, and confusing. But all blessed by God. All of it. Even when the soundtrack doesn't perfectly align with the script.

Reflect & Engage

What are some pieces or genres of music that accompany your life? What role does music play in your spiritual life, whether at church or on your car radio?

KEEPING UP APPEARANCES

Therefore take up the whole armor of God, so that you may be able to withstand on that evil day, and having done everything, to stand firm. —**Ephesians 6:13**

Thirty years ago, I went to California to work on a congressional race. This was back when I did this for a living, so it wasn't *completely* on a whim. When a campaign manager friend called and asked if I'd come out to run the field operation, I figured, "Why not?" My dad had just died, and I was looking for a change of scenery anyway. Of course, as with most campaign jobs, he wanted me there immediately. So I hopped in my dark blue 1985 Ford Bronco II and headed West.

The candidate was a successful divorce lawyer in the East Bay area, but this was the first time he'd ever run for office, so we had some educating to do. For instance, when you're trying to position yourself as a man of the people, and you go knocking on doors in a rougher part of Alameda County, you *probably* shouldn't show up driving a sporty new Mercedes.

I mention this because when we'd argue with this candidate about his choice of car—and he had a lot to choose from— he would always refer to his Mercedes as his "battle vehicle."

It was the car he'd take whenever he had to be in court. That phrase, and more importantly, that mentality, has stuck with me.

Often, we approach life as if we need to wear "battle armor." (Side note: that is what he called the expensive suits he wore to the courthouse.) We want to project an image of strength, power, and great confidence while not allowing anyone to detect even a whiff of insecurity or weakness. We go to great lengths to enter situations on our own terms, with great bravado.

The problem is that this isn't the way to go through life. We can only keep up such images for so long because they don't reflect reality. We are not the images we project; eventually, the walls come a-tumblin' down. Weakness and brokenness, rather than strength and wholeness, more often reflect the reality of our lives.

The life of faith is not about keeping up appearances or projecting images; rather, it's about being open to God, who knows our imperfections and loves us anyway.

To be our most authentic selves, we must allow ourselves to be broken open. And that means putting away our battle vehicles and our power suits and standing naked before God—at least metaphorically—and recognizing that not only are we unable to control every situation, we shouldn't even bother to try. Because it doesn't work. And the only thing we end up battling is our own integrity.

It takes a tremendous amount of energy to maintain an inauthentic image. This energy would be better spent in right relationship with God and those with whom we interact in this life.

So, how did this particular election turn out? Let's just say I was not entirely sorry when we lost a close primary, and I headed back East.

Reflect & Engage

What defenses have you erected to protect your vulnerabilities? What images do you seek to portray that don't mesh with reality? What "armor" might you shed to live a more authentic life?

LIFE IS NOT A HIGHLIGHT REEL

I press on towards the goal for the prize of the heavenly call of God in Christ Jesus.—**Philippians 3:14**

One thing always makes me stop and stare at the TV. It has nothing to do with breaking news. Whether on the treadmill at the gym or walking past the television at home, I get sucked in every time to ESPN's Top 10 Plays of the Week broadcasts.

The thrills and spills of eye-popping athletic achievement never cease to amaze. There's a superhuman quality to these plays, from one-handed grabs in the end zone to fence-leaping catches in center field to high-flying acrobatics above the rim. They're attention-grabbing and exciting, and I can't stop looking until the sportscasters have counted all the way down to the number one top play.

I've always been drawn to the thrill of victory and the agony of defeat, and I suspect I'm not alone. Highlight reels get to the heart of this infatuation without having to wade through the chaff of the rest of the game. These highly curated plays offer us a unique view of sports, and they're fun to watch! But highlights also have a dark side: they distort reality.

One of the great frustrations during my many seasons of coaching Little League baseball was the lack of big-picture

strategic awareness. Perhaps this was a big ask
for a bunch of nine-year-olds. But even the kids who
were huge baseball fans were less interested in hitting
the cutoff man than making the diving highlight-reel catch.

I blame ESPN for this. And our ever-shortening attention
spans. We get bored easily: with relationships, jobs, religion.
So, we switch things up with reckless abandon, expecting
the next great thing will offer hope and fulfillment, which it
rarely, if ever, does.

But life is not a highlight reel. Developing and maintaining
authentic and fulfilling relationships with friends, family,
and God requires hard work. There are many moments of
the mundane, and life itself is full of ordinary time: sitting
with a grieving friend; sipping coffee while reflecting upon
the great mysteries of life; taking a walk through town with
a spouse and dreaming about the future or problem-solving
how to help a child struggling in school.

Of course, our lives have peaks and valleys, highs and lows.
But most of life is lived in the unremarkable in-between
spaces that we likely won't remember next week or next
year. This doesn't mean they are unimportant; indeed, these
times are the bedrock upon which most of our lives are built.
Highlights are important and should rightly be celebrated.
But perhaps we should place equal value on the times when
life isn't as exciting as a reverse slam dunk to win the game
in overtime.

⇨ ⇨ ⇨

Reflect & Engage

What's the balance in your life between highlights and the more mundane moments? How do you mark and celebrate the average times that make up the bulk of your life? How do you define life's highlights?

BLIND SPOTS

You will show me the path of life; in your presence there is fullness of joy, and in your right hand are pleasures for evermore. —**Psalm 16:11**

One of the things about having children is you end up reliving experiences you haven't thought about in years. Sometimes this is a blessing, like when you get to re-watch those original *Star Wars* movies. And sometimes, this is a curse, like when you have to essentially *retake* geometry.

One such experience is learning how to drive. The fits and starts of those early days behind the wheel typically don't come to mind when you hop in the car to run an errand. That is until you have a child taking Driver's Ed, and you suddenly have a driving *expert* sitting next to you. One who criticizes your every rolling stop and comments on your *apparently* lackadaisical use of the blinker.

I've blocked out most of my time in Driver's Ed, but I particularly remember the conversation about the blind spot. Barry, our rather gruff, Brooklyn-bred instructor, seemed to spend a lot of time on it, so I knew that, in theory, there was a spot when changing lanes that you couldn't see by using the mirrors alone. It seemed ridiculous that you couldn't see a big van or truck next to you.

But all it took was driving on the highway for the first time, not completely turning around, and hearing a bus lean on the horn to realize that, oh, *that's* the blind spot Barry was talking about. It's not merely theoretical— and with all the angles involved, maybe geometry is actually useful.

In time, you learn that even beyond driving, we all have blind spots, areas of our lives that we literally can't see. They may have to do with family relationships, politics, or work life. They may be based on our upbringing or gender or race or nationality or faith tradition or socioeconomic class. But these blind spots can wreak havoc on those around us, even if they don't particularly register with us. They're easy enough to ignore until we wind up bumping into something and causing a metaphorical wreck or negatively impacting those around us.

What can we do about our own personal blind spots? One of the best ways is to be in relationship with those who have different perspectives or experiences. When we have conversations with those with whom we disagree or with those whose experiences differ from our own, we expand our field of vision—or at least recognize the existence of our blind spots.

There's a reason that Jesus is always giving sight to the blind. The miracle transcends the physical because the real point is that as our perspective is changed and broadened, we begin to see those on the margins of society, fellow children of God to whom we might otherwise be blind.

In the end, we need assistance in the form of others to help us see our blind spots; we can't do it alone. I encourage you to be open to other viewpoints, to recognize that you don't have all the answers, and to allow the illumination of a new perspective to shine in your heart and soul.

Reflect & Engage

What are some of the blind spots in your life? In what ways are you addressing them? How has increased awareness impacted your life as a person of faith?

SUBJECT TO INTERPRETATION

So shall my word be that goes out from my mouth; it shall not return to me empty, but it shall accomplish that which I purpose, and succeed in the thing for which I sent it. —Isaiah 55:11

Once upon a time, when I was a fraternity pledge, one of the brothers came up to a group of us and demanded that we present to him the lyrics of the song "Louie, Louie." We had one hour to recite them. Or else…well, I don't know what, but something bad.

This 1960s-era classic by The Kingsmen has been played by every garage band that ever played in a fraternity basement, but the lyrics are unintelligible. I mean, nobody has any idea what they are beyond "Louie, Louie," "we gotta go," and "yeah, yeah, yeah, yeah, yeah, yeah." The rest is pure mystery.

This pledge challenge/interaction of brotherly love took place before the magic of the internet. So, ten of us crammed into a dorm room and played the cassette over and over while arguing over the lyrics.

Little did we know that it really didn't matter. No living person, including the lead singer, had any clue about the lyrics. By the time we presented our interpretation to the brother in question, he'd forgotten he'd even asked us in the first place. Such was life as a pledge in the Delta Tau Delta house at Tufts University in the late 1980s.

Interpretation is tricky, whether of lyrics, literature, scripture, and, especially these days, world and national events. We've become so polarized as a nation that it feels like we're speaking completely different languages. Just log onto Facebook and look at your friends' disparate, vehement opinions as Exhibit A of the twisted state of public discourse.

I'm not saying we all have to agree: we're human, after all, with divergent viewpoints and experiences. This kaleidoscope of opinion is the spice of life. But what worries me is that the divisiveness of the interpretation of events has trumped the primacy of our common humanity. From a faith perspective, we have lost sight of the fact that we are, first and foremost, children of God. That's what binds us together and draws us into a sacred wholeness.

As fraternity pledges, we may have argued over the lyrics, disagreed, and even been wrong in our interpretation (we were definitely wrong). But in the end, we were brought together by a common bond. I'm hardly suggesting that a bunch of fraternity boys sent on a fool's errand is a model for lofty dialogue. But the act of how we interpret is valuable if we are to move forward in meaningful ways.

⇨ ⇨ ⇨

Reflect & Engage

How might you be interpreting or misinterpreting the
motives of others during this polarizing time? How might
you be more gracious to those with whom you disagree?
How might you be contributing to the polarization of our
political discourse?

SALTY LANGUAGE

*You must understand this, my beloved: let everyone
be quick to listen, slow to speak, slow to anger; for your
anger does not produce God's righteousness.*
—James 1:19-20

Many years ago, I knew a grizzled priest who had been
an infantryman during the Korean War. He was a faithful
pastor and one of those guys who would literally give
someone the shirt off his back if he met someone in need.
You could always tell when he was around, though, because
he would curse a blue streak. When asked about his salty use
of language, he used to say, "Jesus converted every part of
me except my tongue."

I personally don't curse much, except for a minor
incident when I came home on leave from Fort Knox for
Thanksgiving dinner one year and, midway through the
meal, casually asked my brother to "pass the $*&^#^%
mashed potatoes." That warranted a few raised eyebrows
from the great aunts, but, in my defense, it can be difficult to
extract yourself from the culture in which you're living.

I can't tell you the number of times per week someone
casually curses, notices my clerical collar, and then hastily
apologizes. While some people get incensed by cursing, I'm

not bothered by it, save for places like the local playground or in the middle of worship. I prefer to use old-timey oaths like "criminy!" and "egad!" Partly I do that because they're more socially acceptable but mostly because they're a source of embarrassment when my children overhear me.

I think God has bigger fish to fry than worrying about curse words. Things like poverty and racism, for instance. And I'm pretty sure I do as well.

But the reality is that language is a powerful tool. It can be used to raise up, and it can be used to tear down. There's a difference between cursing as a linguistic device or using it as a throwaway part of speech to belittle or demean someone. The latter is indefensible not because of the particular words themselves but because of the attitude behind them. When we curse at someone, we actively minimize their value as a fellow child of God. In my book, that's a lot different than saying a bad word when you hit your thumb with a hammer.

This naturally brings up the matter of taking the Lord's name in vain, which has apparently been going on since humanity first learned God's name. I mean, there's a reason this prohibition made the original Top 10 list, aka the 10 Commandments. The negative things we say about God and one another matter because, as Jesus put it, "the things that come out of the mouth defile." Why? Because they are a reflection of the heart. There's usually a story behind our words and how we use them. These stories transcend words and expose our souls' most profound dreams, desires, and hurts.

I'll be honest: it feels good to occasionally let loose a string of socially forbidden words. A few recent studies even claim cursing is a good stress reliever. Apparently, these studies say there's a point of diminishing returns: those who curse regularly don't benefit as much as those who choose their spots more judiciously.

Either way, I won't be too offended the next time I overhear you say something salty when your car won't start. You don't even need to apologize.

Reflect & Engage

Think about your own use of curse words. How often do they infiltrate your vocabulary, and in what ways? What does your use of them say about your heart?

STAYING FOCUSED

Then the LORD answered me and said: Write the vision; make it plain on tablets, so that a runner may read it. —Habakkuk 2:2

Many years ago, when I shared with a particular friend that I was going to seminary to pursue ordained ministry, he immediately said, "That's great! From now on, anything bad that happens to you can end up in a sermon."

Well, hopefully, that's not entirely true. I try to keep my dirty laundry in the hamper rather than the pulpit. But occasionally, things that happen to me end up in sermons I preach or columns I write since they ideally reflect an intersection between real life and authentic faith.

All of which is to say I recently passed a midlife milestone: I now wear bifocals. You can call them "progressive lenses" to make me feel better. And while I do consider myself to be a relatively progressive person, I guess this beats wearing "reactionary lenses." No one at the optical store even offered me a pair of rose-colored glasses.

But the term "progressive lenses" still feels like language meant to soothe the ego rather than reflect the reality of the aging process. It's kind of like calling it a "funeral home"

instead of a "place to warehouse dead people."
I mean, no one actually lives in this alleged "home,"
as far as I know.

I definitely had an adjustment period to my new lenses.
There were extra typos when writing emails, and, truth be
told, they made me feel slightly drunk, especially on stairs.

Perspective is, of course, an important theme in life, perhaps
especially in our spiritual lives. It is perspective that allows
us to embrace an attitude of gratitude. It is perspective
that allows us to see the hand of God at work in our daily
encounters. It is perspective that encourages us to reach out
to those in need or trouble.

The filter, or lens, through which we view the world matters.
New sight lines emerge when we take the time to see life
through the divine perspective. The colors of God's creation
become brighter, and we're offered a stunning vista of
human hope and possibility.

Of course, embracing faith has something else in common
with bifocals. You keep your original perspective while
adding a new one, the divine lens, if you will. And while you
occasionally stumble, faith ultimately allows you to see even
more clearly. Soon enough, as with breaking in a new pair of
glasses, this transformed perspective becomes such a part of
you that you can't imagine life without it.

It didn't take too long to get used to my new glasses. The hardest part was trying to find the sweet spot to see the altar book on Sunday morning. And now that I have attained this middle-aged rite of passage, I'm ready for the next milestone. Who's up for a knee replacement?

Reflect & Engage

How has your perspective changed over the years? What's more important to you in this decade of your life than the last one or previous ones? Name a life-changing event that helped change your perspective. In what ways did it change?

SEEING THE BIG PICTURE

For now we see in a mirror, dimly, but then we will see face to face. —Corinthians 13:12

When I was a kid, my parents often dragged me and my brother to museums. They weren't trying to ram culture down our throats; they were genuinely inspired by art and wanted to share that passion with their children. But we were kids, and we whined and complained our way through centuries of magnificent works of art until we reached the great pinnacle of the museum experience: the gift shop.

Despite my disregard for most things museum, I remember being fascinated with one particular style of painting known as pointillism. That's the medium in which artists place small distinct dots in patterns that ultimately make images. When you stand close, all you see is a bunch of dots. But as you back up, the figures and background begin to emerge. At a certain distance, you can no longer even tell that there are any dots. They blend together to form what looks like a typical painting.

Perhaps the most famous example of pointillism is the late-nineteenth-century Georges Seurat painting "A Sunday Afternoon on the Island of La Grande Jatte." It hangs in the Art Institute of Chicago, a place I went to (of my own accord!) a few times while attending seminary in Chicago. They have a *great* gift shop, by the way.

I was thinking about this recently as it relates to our lives. So often, we focus on the dots and miss the big picture. We get annoyed with our children for spending too much time on the Xbox rather than giving thanks for the gift of their very existence. We get frustrated with the time it takes to attend to the needs of aging parents rather than being grateful for their continued presence in our lives. We focus on doing the dishes rather than enjoying the company of our guests.

As with encountering a pointillist painting, it's important to take a step back to see the big picture of our lives, even as the details and annoyances of the everyday continually draw us in. Otherwise, we will get to the end of our lives and realize we weren't paying attention to what, in the end, matters. To paraphrase Bill Clinton's slogan on the economy, "It's about the relationships, stupid."

Seeing the big picture hinges on gratitude and thanksgiving. This posture of faith is a way of viewing life as a gift from God rather than something to endure or "get through." God pulls us back, away from the dots of life, allowing us to see things in all their glorious living color. And when we let God do this, the full image of God's love for us becomes increasingly clear.

I still love museum gift shops. And while I no longer see them as sweet relief from the cruel and unusual punishment of being exposed to art, my kids sure do.

⇨ ⇨ ⇨

Reflect & Engage:

In what ways do you focus on the dots of your life while failing to see the big picture? Is there an area in your life where you wish you were better at cultivating gratitude?

NAVIGATING ROUGH WATERS

Jesus woke up and rebuked the wind, and said to the sea, "Peace! Be still!" Then the wind ceased, and there was a dead calm. —**Mark 4:39**

The comedian Steven Wright once said, "You know when you're sitting on a chair, and you lean back, so you're just on two legs, and you lean too far, so you almost fall over, but at the last second, you catch yourself? I feel like that all the time..."

We may not feel like this *all the time*, but all of us have experienced the feeling of being unsettled, particularly around transitions as we move from one phase to another. I remember feeling this way when our kids were in school, and the calendar suddenly flipped from Labor Day to the first day of school. Overnight, we shifted from lollygagging to boot camp.

There are few such dramatic transitions in life than the one from summer to school year. Whether or not we have kids in school, we all vividly remember that movement from lazy days to calendar routines, from hearing the dinner bell summoning us back from an evening of playing with friends to the school bell calling us to the next class.

Much of life is lived amid transitions that take periods of adjustment. When a loved one dies, it takes time to enter the new reality without this person. When we start a new job, as excited as we may be, we often spend the first week in a bit of shellshock, reeling from all the information coming our way.

I once went kayaking with a friend in the waning days of August. It was a beautiful, if breezy, day, and our plan was to go under a bridge leading from the harbor into the ocean. He'd been out there before and promised scenic views of the coastline and the grand houses along the waterfront. Things were going swimmingly until we noticed some white water under the bridge. It looked a little rough, but we were ready to attack the current and head out to the open water. Full steam ahead!

Well, things didn't quite go as planned. In an instant, we were dumped into the drink. Visions of Davy Jones's locker danced in my head as I scrambled to grab hold of the boat and look for my friend. Once we realized we were both fine (the only thing lost at sea were his sunglasses and our collective dignity) and it was just a matter of letting the current take us to a nearby island, we were able to relax and devise a story so our wives wouldn't laugh at us too much.

The point is that our situations can change in a moment. Sometimes we see it coming—the Tuesday after Labor

Day looms on the calendar for weeks—and sometimes it catches us off-guard, as when a boating trip turns into an impromptu swim.

You can learn some lessons along the way, like not trying to go out to sea near high tide. But sometimes, you just have to go with the flow, knowing that anticipated and unexpected transitions are part of life. Give yourself a break and be intentional about easing into them. And know that God is with you at every step, or stroke, of the way.

Reflect & Engage

What are some transitions you've experienced recently? Were they jarring or smooth? What strategies did you employ to manage them?

PARDON THE INTERRUPTION

But finding no way to bring him in because of the crowd, they went up on the roof and let him down with his bed through the tiles into the middle of the crowd in front of Jesus. —**Luke 5:19**

There's a show on ESPN called *Pardon the Interruption*, which gives me agita. This roundup of the day's sports news is hosted by a couple of loud, contentious talking heads with strongly voiced opinions about…everything. It's like the sports version of the McLaughlin Group, the long-running PBS news show that puts liberals and conservatives around a table and lets them have at it. Both shows are 30 minutes of people interrupting one another in what is basically a verbal food fight.

Much of ministry, like life itself, is an interruption. You map out your day, yet it often veers off in a completely different direction. Those plans you had to write the newsletter article? That gets trumped when you get a phone call saying someone took a fall and is being transported to the local hospital. Or the time you carved out to sit in your office and go over the budget for an upcoming meeting? That goes out the window when a parishioner comes in with news that her father just died.

You can either rue the disruption of your regular routine, or you can view it as an opportunity to serve others. And you learn quickly that people are much more important than your calendar, deadlines, or to-do list.

Jesus certainly knew what it was to get interrupted. During his brief, what I like to call "rock star" phase when people hounded him wherever he went, his life was one long interruption. He couldn't go anywhere without people clamoring for his attention, a healing touch, or a chance to take a selfie. If he wanted a quiet moment for renewal, he had to slip away by the cover of darkness to find a place to pray—and even then, people caught up with him and interrupted his private devotions with their own needs and concerns. Yet, despite all these interruptions, Jesus never complained.

In fact, Jesus's approach to interruptions can help us shift our perspective. Instead of viewing interruptions as sources of annoyance and frustration, we can begin to thank God for what I call "holy interruptions," unplanned interactions with others that make a difference in our own lives or those of others.

The challenge is that we have to be open to the holy interruptions that present themselves. Sometimes this means putting our phones away and really listening. It means seeing the divine in others even when we'd rather not get involved. It means being flexible as we go about our days: flexible enough to leave room for people who may be hurting or vulnerable or seeking a word of comfort from a friend or stranger. It means cultivating awareness of those in our midst rather than remaining inwardly focused.

I encourage you to reflect on the possibilities for such holy interruptions in your life. Don't pardon the interruption but embrace it. Allow interruptions to instruct rather than disrupt. And know that your life will be all the richer for it.

Reflect & Engage

Name a time you've encountered a holy interruption. In what ways did it change the course of your day?

WAIT: WHY AM I TALKING?

Even fools who keep silent are considered wise; when they close their lips, they are deemed intelligent.
—**Proverbs** 17:28

I had lunch with a parishioner recently who told me about an acronym he had learned at a business seminar. It was WAIT; it stood for "Why Am I Talking?" When you're a preacher, you're used to people wondering this about you. But the basic premise is a reminder to talk less and listen more.

This good advice didn't just spring up as the latest business catchphrase. The ancient Greek philosopher Epictetus proclaimed, "We have two ears and one mouth, so we can listen twice as much as we speak." Author Mark Twain offered the corollary: "If we were meant to talk more than listen, we would have two mouths and one ear."

Many of us find ourselves in vocations, family interactions, or social situations where we are expected to talk. It comes with being a leader, an expert, a teacher, a parent, or just a polite member of society. But in these roles, we sometimes feel the need to speak because we think that's what others expect. We find ourselves talking just for the sake of talking, sometimes drowning out other voices and perspectives from which we could learn.

The idea of the acronym WAIT is to speak only when we have something to contribute. It also helps to recognize that we're not God's gift to the conversation, whether in the boardroom, at the dinner table, or on the telephone.

In the same vein, we often spend time in conversations formulating what we plan to say rather than listening to others. This happens in classrooms, Bible studies, work meetings, and volunteer committees. In our effort to sound eloquent and project the right image, we stop listening to others. We ignore actual interaction, and the conversation devolves into a bunch of individual monologues.

From a faith perspective, this concept of asking ourselves, "Why am I talking?" also applies to our prayer lives. Generally speaking, when we pray, we're yappers. We talk way too much. We try to name every person we've ever met or every situation we can think of that needs healing. We mentally run through our world atlas, thinking hard about all the hotspots where there's war, conflict, or natural disaster. We try to remember all the tragedies we've heard about on the news in the last 24 hours. Or our friends on Facebook who broke legs, lost jobs, or had kids home sick from school. The list goes on and on and on, with the end result being guilt when we realize we forgot to pray for Aunt Millie's upcoming procedure to remove that pesky toe fungus.

Praying for others is important, of course. But we can get so caught up in telling God what to do that we neglect the most vital part of prayer, which is listening. And we forget that God already knows all our needs before we ask.

I don't know about you, but that takes a lot of pressure off. I don't have to run down the shopping list of prayer requests, fearing that I'll forget to pray for peace in the Middle East or those suffering from flooding in Missouri.

The next time you hear yourself nattering on—internally or externally—ask yourself, "Why Am I Talking?" Sometimes silence truly is golden.

Reflect & Engage

Can you think of a situation where you spoke too much? How might you have approached the situation differently?

DIRTY WORK

Whatever your task, put yourselves into it, as done for the Lord and not for your masters. —**Colossians 3:23**

No, I didn't actually put it on a scale. But on the first warm day after a long winter, I must have picked up 20 pounds of dog poop. I know what you're thinking. "Tim, don't you have two boys to do this?" Yes. Yes, I do. However, if I wanted it picked up before the Fourth of July, it was easier to do it myself.

As I bent down again and again, watching my step at every turn, I rued not doing this while it was all still frozen. I also envied our two dogs, who were the source of all this…stuff, as they sunned themselves while I did the dirty work.

But after a few minutes of grumbling, something changed. The fact is, I was enjoying myself. After a long winter, just being outside was a source of joy. Perhaps there was some activity that would have been a drag on a beautiful day, but I think even grave digging would have put a spring in my step as the temperature moved into the mid-60s.

I'm no philosopher of feces, but the experience reminded me that finding joy amidst drudgery is one of the keys to happiness. Saint Benedict, the sixth-century "Father of Western Monasticism," encouraged his monks to view everything they did, no matter how outwardly mundane, as an act of worship, whether tilling the soil, washing dishes, or making the bed. I have no idea whether Saint Benedict's monks kept dogs (Saint Bernards?), but if so, surely the same concept would apply to poop patrol.

I'm not planning to add picking up dog poop to the Sunday morning liturgy at church. I won't send everyone out to the backyard of the rectory just after the first reading to experience such a holy act. But I am reminded that shifting our perspective, even slightly, can allow joy to slip into our lives in unexpected ways.

Benedict took this concept further by helping his monks see that every implement or tool they used was a holy object. A rake, when used to the glory of God, was just as special as the silver chalice used to serve communion wine at the altar. It may be difficult to see that plastic Stop & Shop bag I used to collect my dogs' "offerings" as something sacred, but I'll keep trying.

Reflect & Engage

What obligatory act in your life might be a window into an unexpected encounter with God? What menial or mindless task might be repurposed to change your perspective in a positive way?

DRAWING IT UP

For my thoughts are not your thoughts, nor are your ways my ways, says the Lord. —Isaiah 55:8

Things don't always go according to plan. That's no great newsflash to anyone who's lived for more than, oh, about two minutes. You might have preferred to keep that umbilical cord intact. But cord-cutting was just the first of a lifetime of challenges to preferred outcomes.

We tend to create a vision of how we see our lives unfolding—and then it plays out the way it plays out. That's not to say we have no control at all, but unforeseen circumstances are part of life, and our ability to adapt and improvise often separates personal satisfaction from bitter disappointment.

After a busted play ends up going for a long gain, football commentators often say, with the unnuanced irony of the ex-jock, "Well, that's just how they drew it up." Sometimes a pass hits a receiver in the helmet and bounces right into the hands of a teammate. Great! But you can't put that identical play into next week's game plan.

We don't "draw up" things like the death of a loved one or a divorce or a child with special needs or financial instability or addiction or a mental health crisis. That's not part of the vision for the life that we have so carefully laid out. But these things happen, and the first, perfectly understandable, response is often shame or anger.

These unexpected, painful, busted plays of life are inevitable: they are part of the human condition. The good news for people of faith is the knowledge that God is present through them all, standing beside us, comforting us, strengthening us, weeping with us. That doesn't make painful things magically disappear, but it gives us the confidence to move forward, however haltingly.

One year, the boiler at my New England church breathed its last just as the weather was starting to turn colder. Great timing, right? Okay, there's *never* a good time for the boiler to die, but we were hoping to get another couple of years out of the old beast before having to fund a new one.

Things don't always work out the way you drew them up in the locker room of life. And sometimes you just have to shake your head, laugh at the absurdity of the situation, and host a Boilermaker Party to raise money for the new boiler (that's a shot of whiskey dropped into a beer, if I remember correctly from my fraternity days).

In the end, it all comes down to asking, "Is this my plan for God or God's plan for me?" It's human hubris to think we're in charge of things because, frankly, we're not. The sooner we recognize this, the more peace and perspective we'll have when the inevitable darker moments of our lives arise.

Go ahead and plan. But then take the detours and obstacles that arise and live your life fully and joyfully, even if you have to put on an extra layer when the boiler dies.

Reflect & Engage

What unanticipated twists and turns have happened throughout your life? In what ways were you able to adapt and see the hand of God?

ROAD TRIP

But a Samaritan while traveling came near him;
and when he saw him, he was moved with pity.
—Luke 10:33

The most memorable road trip I took was driving from
Maryland to California. By myself. In three days.

This was back in my early 20s, so I was young and, if not
stupid, at least energetic. I was offered a job in the East Bay
area that started, well, as soon as possible. So, I hopped in
my vehicle and hit the road. This was long before cell phones
and satellite radio and GPS, so it was just me, my AM/FM
radio, and a bunch of maps for 3,000 miles. I listened to a lot
of country music and pulpit-pounding, fire-and-brimstone
preachers. The third option was static.

The only real snafu was breaking down outside Omaha,
Nebraska, and spending five hours in a gas station awaiting
the arrival of a new fuel pump. I was glad I wasn't driving a
Subaru or a Volvo since, if it took five hours to find a *Ford*
part, I'd probably still be waiting.

One of the things my children can't and won't ever be able to
relate to is being stranded on the side of the road. "What do
you mean you couldn't just use your cell phone to call a tow
truck?" They have trouble understanding that in the olden

days, if you blew out a tire or your car overheated on a dark and lonely stretch of highway, you just had to pull over to the shoulder and wait. Since there was no cell phone safety net for always being in touch, you were literally at the mercy of some "good Samaritan" who happened to pull over to help.

For those who can barely remember the time before our current era of hyper-connectivity or who never experienced it, a better analogy might be those times in our lives when we feel emotionally and spiritually cut off. Even though the internet offers us the entire world at our fingertips, there are still moments when we feel disconnected and isolated, when we feel as if we're standing on the side of the road with nary a car in sight, when "no signal" isn't about our data plan but our very souls.

It's moments like these when we realize our devices can only take us so far in life. To thrive, we need to experience joy and fruitful relationships. And that's something we can't do alone. We need the company of others, and, most importantly, we need divine connection.

The good news is that God never abandons us or leaves us stranded or refuses to listen when we cry out. And nothing we do or fail to do can ever separate us from God's love for us. Sure, we sometimes run out of spiritual gas along the road of life, but God is always there to offer comfort, solace, strength, and continuing relationship.

⇨ ⇨ ⇨

Reflect & Engage

Can you recall a time when you were stranded on the side of the road? How did it make you feel? Where do you find God when you feel physically or emotionally abandoned?

SHIFTING PERSPECTIVES

Such great crowds gathered around him that he got into a boat and sat there, while the whole crowd stood on the beach. —**Matthew 13:2**

One of the great gifts of having children is being drawn into their passions and interests, especially things you would never have discovered on your own. I often think about my late father, a symphony orchestra conductor with no interest in sports, who used to come to my Little League games. Over the years, he developed a genuine love of baseball, and we spent many splendid afternoons watching the Orioles together at the old Memorial Stadium in Baltimore.

One summer, I received a similar gift from my own children. During a family outing, the boys decided to try sea kayaking. They went out in a two-person tandem, and while they nearly came to blows with the paddles, accusing one another of not "pulling your weight," they both decided they wanted to try it again—in single-person kayaks.

We were fortunate to live near the water, with two local kayak rental places. So off they went for an hour kayaking around the harbor, and, miracle of miracles, they got along famously out on the water. Stepping back onto dry land was another matter, but they both took to kayaking like, well, boats to water.

After renting kayaks a bunch of times, it didn't take a financial wizard to figure out it would be cheaper to buy our own. The next thing I knew, we had a kayak rack on our SUV. At first, I thought we should stick with the rack and forget the kayaks since it made us look so sporty driving around town.

But a funny thing happened along the way: I got hooked. When I went out with the boys, I immediately saw the attraction: good exercise, peaceful, scenic, and a great way to spend quality time with the kids away from phones, laptops, video game consoles, and televisions. It's tough to text and paddle. I started reading books about kayaking and anticipating the next voyage as much as the boys.

Eventually, I found a used kayak on Craig's List that looked promising, and suddenly we were owners of the SS Schenck. It's an orange and yellow 12 ½-foot kayak with a couple of storage hatches just big enough for a six-pack, I mean, picnic basket.

We learned some lessons along the way: for instance, wet boats are slippery. I broke the side mirror off my wife's car after the boat slipped from the rack following the maiden voyage in Hingham Harbor. The repair cost as much as the second kayak we needed. We also learned the hard way that low tide is a lousy time to kayak.

What I have come to love most about kayaking is the new perspective I've gained. I had never seen my town from the water, and it's stunning: the small islands, the boats dancing in the harbor. Sometimes a shift in perspective is just what we need to reclaim grateful hearts and renew our faith. I'm thankful to Ben and Zak for this gift, even if we lost a side mirror in the process.

Reflect & Engage

What passion or hobby have you been given by a younger person? How did it come about? How has this changed your perspective?

LEAP OF FAITH

Now faith is the assurance of things hoped for, the conviction of things not seen. —**Hebrews 11:1**

What is your greatest fear? Spiders? Ghosts? Confined spaces? Clowns? If pushed, we can all come up with at least a few things that give us the willies.

I was thinking about my greatest fear recently: heights. Of course, fear is one thing, but how you deal with it can be a commentary on faith. In my case, I decided to lean into my fear of heights rather than avoid it. Thirty-five years ago, I found myself at Fort Benning, Georgia, having volunteered to go to Airborne School. At the time, I was an Army ROTC cadet attending Tufts University, and, being afraid of heights, I decided I needed to jump out of a perfectly good airplane.

The scariest training apparatus/torture device I encountered was called the 34-foot tower, where you learn the proper technique to exit the aircraft. Why 34 feet? Because Army engineers determined this was the precise height where fear was maximized: you're not so high up that everything on the ground looks fake, and you're not so low that it looks safe. When it's your turn, you get hooked up to a harness and free fall about four feet before your line catches and yanks you back to a zip line.

During the third week, if you make it that far,
you have to take five jumps to qualify for your
Airborne wings. When you're actually in the airplane
and standing at the door, it's loud and windy; suddenly
the green light goes on, and you leap out into what feels like
the abyss. It is quite literally a leap of faith.

Isn't this what the spiritual life feels like some days? We're all
working without a net, seeking to confront our fears, seeking
to do our best. It's important to remember that even amid
fear, the divine is present. Even when we feel God-forsaken,
we're not. This doesn't mean we never succumb to our fears,
but it does mean God is in the midst of our failures as well as
our successes, and there is comfort in that knowledge.

After you leap out into that violent rush of wind and your
parachute opens up, the contrasting silence and peacefulness
of the descent are remarkable. Of course, the ground starts
to come up rather quickly, so you can't stay in this state of
reverie for very long.

The ground reminds us that faith isn't just about an
individual, personal spiritual experience. We take the
experience and hit the ground running: sharing our
faith with others; opening our hearts to one another, and
becoming part of a faith community that acts as God's
hands and heart in the world.

Fortunately for me, this all takes place on *terra firma* because, while I know I can deal with my fears if I must, I still don't like heights.

⇨ ⇨ ⇨

Reflect & Engage

What is your greatest fear, and how have you interacted with it over the years? In interacting with your fear, have you encountered God's presence? In what ways?

CREATURE OF HABIT

Therefore be imitators of God, as beloved children, and live in love, as Christ loved us and gave himself up for us, a fragrant offering and sacrifice to God.
—Ephesians 5:1-2

Ever since I learned to read, I've started each day with a bowl of cereal and the sports section. I keep this up because a) Lucky Charms are "magically delicious," and b) I much prefer to begin the day with the escapism of sports than the reality of human suffering. While I guess this makes me a creature of habit, I don't think that's such a bad thing. We all crave routines that bring comfort and help order our lives. Mine just happens to involve reading about my beloved sad-sack Baltimore Orioles.

When you reflect upon all you do on a regular basis, you soon realize there are many daily rituals. These may revolve around coffee, an exercise routine, or even how you load and unload the dishwasher (knives down, spoons up!). Routines ease the chaos of our fast-paced lives and help ground our daily existence.

I've come to see ritual as an innate function of our humanity. Children are drawn to repetition and find comfort in the familiar. Just ask any parent about the vaunted "bedtime routine." While these vary slightly from home to home, they generally involve multiple cups of water, reading *Goodnight Moon ad nauseum*, and profound questions just when you're ready to collapse ("Mom, why does God cause earthquakes?").

Children deeply crave ritual. For them and all of us, it creates a sense of safety, comfort, and order. We put our pants on the same way every morning so we don't have to think about it; we do a crossword puzzle every night before turning out the light so our eyes know when it's time to droop; we go to the same mechanic for an oil change every few months.

Religious ritual is a routine of both power and comfort. When a member of the Jewish community dies, friends and family sit Shiva. Whether a death is expected or sudden, ritual kicks in, strictly defining the hours and days that follow. This brings holy order to what can be a time of bewildering chaos.

The danger with the routine of ritual is that it can become rote. For many, the Lord's Prayer falls into this category. How many times have you said it without thinking about the power of Jesus's words? The prayer rolls off the tongue like the Pledge of Allegiance or the alphabet, but to truly pray the Lord's Prayer takes intentionality. And yet even when we are just saying the words, something is happening. I've been with many people on their deathbeds who, while seemingly "out of it," mouth the words of the Lord's Prayer when I pray it with them. Ritual runs deep in our souls.

Being a creature of habit is not a bad thing. As long as our routines don't become obsessive, they are imbued with comfort—even when they involve reading yet another losing box score and bemoaning the fact that you're way too old to eat Lucky Charms.

Reflect & Engage

What rituals bring you comfort? What is the role of religious ritual in your life? In what ways does ritual keep you grounded?

BUZZ KILL

Listen to me, you who know righteousness, you people who have my teaching in your hearts; do not fear the reproach of others, and do not be dismayed when they revile you. —**Isaiah 51:7**

I grudgingly admit that mosquitoes are God's creatures. I guess they fall into the "small" category of "All creatures great and small." But let's face it, God has done better work. From a scientific point of view, I suppose these flying leeches serve some purpose in the wider ecosystem. I can't imagine what it is, though. "Here, take my blood, make my skin itch like crazy, and then leave me with a potentially deadly virus. Thanks!"

About a month ago, I killed a mosquito while preaching a sermon on a Sunday morning. It was buzzing around my head, and with cat-like reflexes, I reached out and nabbed it between my thumb and forefinger. With my left hand, I might add. This led to several practical and ethical questions: what do you do with a squished mosquito between your fingers while in the pulpit? Does killing one of God's creatures while preaching the Word of God invalidate the sermon? Does it mean I'm failing to practice what I preach?

We all have pests in our lives. Some have wings and suck our blood, while others are just annoying and passive aggressive. It's not un-Christian to admit that some people drive you nuts. We all have crosses to bear (although let's not confuse the redemptive power of the cross of Christ with a whiny cousin). The beauty of God's creation is in its depth and breadth.

How we treat the pests we encounter in this life says a lot about our character. Jesus tells us to love our enemies, but he doesn't say much about those who drive us crazy. It's hard to love the neighbor who mows his lawn at 6 a.m. on a Sunday morning or the joker who drives 48 miles per hour in the left lane. We can try to swat them away or put the squeeze on them or set up a bug zapper (though that may be less effective on your Uncle Bob). But maybe we should try a different approach: if we can't love them, we can at least try to coexist with them. There will always be pests among us, whether they come in mosquito form or human flesh. If you drive one away, others are itching to take their place.

While mosquitoes are annoying, we don't let them ruin our entire summer. We have coping mechanisms like bug spray and screen doors and letting our spouse take the kid to the travel league baseball game. In the same way, we can't let human mosquitoes ruin our lives. Coping mechanisms include praying for those who annoy us, breathing deeply, and keeping things in perspective. And remember: at least they can't give us the West Nile Virus.

Now about that squished mosquito in the pulpit. I couldn't continue preaching with a dead bug in my hand; I have some standards. I ended up letting its corpse float to the ground while muttering something about being glad it wasn't St. Francis Day.

Reflect & Engage

What (or who) are the pests in your life? What coping mechanisms do you have to coexist with them? What have you learned about God through your encounters with them?

CHANCE ENCOUNTERS

But God proves his love for us in that while we still were sinners Christ died for us. —**Romans 5:8**

I recently traveled to Kentucky for the first time in many years. Being in the Bluegrass State reminded me of my last encounter with Kentucky. After college, I spent four months at Fort Knox training to be a tank platoon leader. Some days, I swear this was better training for parish ministry than studying theology, but that's another matter.

Anyway, Route 31 in Kentucky connects the city of Louisville to Fort Knox, and I traveled this road on a regular basis whenever we'd have weekends off. Route 31 was nothing if not nondescript, but I distinctly remember passing a particular business establishment. It was a liquor store just outside the county line between dry Bullitt County, where the sale of alcohol was prohibited, and wet Hardin County, where alcohol sales were legal.

Driving down Route 31 through the dry county and approaching the wet one, the liquor store's giant neon sign read "Benny's First Chance." But when you traveled the opposite way on Route 31, through the wet county approaching the dry one, the giant neon sign read "Benny's Last Chance." This clever marketing ploy has probably served Benny well over the years, and it's certainly stuck in my mind.

From a spiritual perspective, we're offered several first—and last—chances. Every day in every moment, we're offered a first chance to turn our hearts to God. The door is always open, the arms are always wide, the welcoming embrace is always offered, and the invitation always stands. Sometimes, that first step into genuine relationship feels like stepping off a cliff; it's called a leap of faith, after all. But letting go is part of living into that first chance to be with the divine. And this is a chance we're asked to take again and again and again.

Last chances are trickier. A last chance feels like an ultimatum: "Turn to God or else..." Preachers have fed off the fear of the last chance for generations, and while it's occasionally effective in keeping people in line or coming through the doors, I don't believe this approach gets to the heart of God. Coming face-to-face with the last chance of God's judgment is always within the context of God's loving mercy. The merciful judgment of God demands that we take God up on the first chances we're continually offered to serve God and one another. Regardless of whether it's a first chance or a last chance, we're always encouraged to take a chance on God's love.

$\Rightarrow \Rightarrow \Rightarrow$

Reflect & Engage

When did you take a chance on God, whether through
an encounter with another person or a decision you made?
In what ways has God taken a chance on you?

FILL DIRT

But as for what was sown on good soil, this is the one who hears the word and understands it, who indeed bears fruit and yields, in one case a hundredfold, in another sixty, and in another thirty. —**Matthew 13:23**

Cleanliness may or may not be next to godliness, but dirt undoubtedly plays an oversized role in our lives. From Adam being created from the dust of the earth to making mud pies as children to mowing the lawn as an adult, we have many points of contact with dirt throughout our lives. And that doesn't even include that disgusting statistic about how many pounds of dirt we consume in a lifetime (for the record, it's six pounds. Gross).

For those of us who are neither farmers nor landscapers, we tend to see dirt as something monolithic. We don't spend much time thinking about the different kinds or properties of dirt. Dirt primarily exists as something to avoid on our bodies. We may admire our neighbor's rhododendron, but we don't give much thought to what lies beneath the surface.

Yet, in a very real sense, the soil of our lives is like fill dirt. That's the dirt that's taken from one construction site where holes are being dug, perhaps to put in a pool or excavate for a building's foundation, and taken to another site where earth is needed for regrading or landscaping. Sometimes you'll see signs around town at houses where construction is being done: "Free Fill Dirt" or "Fill Dirt Wanted." Basically, fill dirt is the unwanted dirt of the soil world, getting repurposed and reused and moved from project to project. It's necessary, but it's not pure in any form. There's often some good soil mixed in, along with rocks and sand and weeds.

We like to think our receptivity to God is more like a bag of potting soil from Home Depot—rich earth, chock-full of nutrients specifically engineered to encourage the greatest growth. That's what you sink your geraniums into or use when you plant sweet-smelling herbs like basil or lavender. We like to think that because we attend church and say our prayers or occasionally pick up the Bible, we are always receptive to the moving of God's spirit in our lives. And we often are—but not always. Sometimes we do all the right things to nurture our faith, yet nothing takes root. Other times, we do nothing to put ourselves in a particularly prayerful posture, and we suddenly have a powerful and surprising encounter with God. These experiences lead us to understand that we're not the ones actually in control here. We have a role to play in the process of spiritual growth, but it often happens in ways that are well beyond our control.

The reality is that our lives are made up of a patchwork of different soils. We bear fruit in different quantities at different times. Some days, we're particularly receptive to hearing God's Word and acting on it; on other days, it gets choked out by the pressing concerns and distractions of our over-scheduled lives. Some days, we don't understand or can't hear God's Word; on other days, we receive it joyfully, but it doesn't stick. This might remind you of Jesus's well-known parable of the sower.

The next time you prepare to scrub the dirt off your hands after an intense session of gardening or a game of touch football, give a passing thought to the dirt itself and consider your own receptivity to God's vision for you.

Reflect & Engage

How has your experience with dirt brought you into contact with God? Name a time when you felt particularly receptive to the moving of God's spirit in your life.

TUNING PEG

But as for you, return to your God, hold fast to
love and justice, and wait continually for your God.
—Hosea 12:6

When I was a kid, I would sometimes tag along with my
father to orchestra rehearsals. He was a conductor with
the Baltimore Symphony Orchestra in the 1970s, and so
when a babysitter got sick or my mother was working, I'd
accompany my dad to the old Lyric Theater downtown.
When I wasn't hanging out in the dressing room with the
poker-playing horn players or wandering backstage among
the huge double bass cases and assorted timpanis, I'd be out
exploring the red velvet-lined boxes in the balcony.

You could say that one of the soundtracks of my childhood
was the tuning of the orchestra. If you've ever been to a
classical music concert, you know that they all start with
the same ritual tuning. After a nod from the concertmaster,
the principal oboe player gives them an A, and then the
rest of the orchestra tunes their instruments off of the oboe,
which, of all the instruments, provides the truest pitch. This
process takes just a few moments, but the tune-up starts the
rehearsal and then is repeated periodically if the conductor
hears something that doesn't sound quite right.

Over time, instruments naturally get out of tune if left alone. Strings, in particular, are very sensitive to cold or humidity. A violin string might stretch out, causing it to go flat or constrict, causing it to go sharp. And so a violinist must do a bit of finetuning with the pegs to get the instrument back in playing condition.

We, too, occasionally find ourselves out of tune spiritually. As our priorities become slightly off-key, it's important for us to find ways to again live in harmony with God. The truth is that it's easy to let our spiritual lives get away from us. We get busy; we get self-absorbed; we get bogged down by endless activities. We let the minutiae of life drive our priorities, and suddenly we find ourselves out of tune with the Spirit. It might be subtle to the point that we hardly notice our spiritual life has gone a bit flat. Or it might be strident, atonal disharmony. But either way, we need to seek ways to bring our spiritual lives back into tune through self-reflection and a return to the basics of our faith.

Pay attention to the occasional need to retune your spiritual life. Needing tweaks is a natural phenomenon that affects even the most devout among us. We can't fix everything in our lives or in the world. But we can attend to the stirrings of our souls. And by doing so, we can be bearers of God's grace in uncertain moments. We can drive out fear with hope. We can offer love in the face of oppression. This is what will transform us: being in tune with God and walking in harmony with one another.

⇨ ⇨ ⇨

Reflect & Engage

Describe a moment or a season when you felt spiritually out of tune. How did you retune your spiritual life?

ANGEL'S SHARE

Bless the LORD, *you angels of his, you mighty ones who do his bidding, and hearken to the voice of his word.*
—Psalm 103:20

One summer, when I was back home in Baltimore visiting family, we toured a whiskey distillery. This may seem like an odd family outing, especially since only two of the five cousins were actually of legal drinking age, but it was a rainy day, and we needed an indoor activity. So after breakfast, we headed down to the Sagamore Spirit Distillery in South Baltimore.

I didn't realize that before Prohibition, Maryland was the rye whiskey capital of America. The industry didn't consolidate into Kentucky until after World War II. Maryland-style whiskey was a thing, and several boutique distilleries are seeking to bring it back. Baltimore scribe and whiskey enthusiast H.L. Mencken was a big fan, calling Maryland whiskey "the most healthful appetizer known to man."

We can debate that, but I find the process of distilling spirits both fascinating and mysterious. The mashing and malting, fermenting and aging is part science project and part art form, often conducted by large apron-wearing bearded men. But the aspect I love the most happens inside those wooden barrels. As part of the aging process, a small percentage of the liquid evaporates. In fact, 2% of what's inside the barrel evaporates for every year that it's aged.

This is both a blessing and a curse. It means that a portion of the whiskey is lost, but it's only through the aging process that the whiskey develops its unique flavor and character.

Distillers refer to this lost portion of whiskey that dissipates into the heavens as the "angel's share." I love this phrase. It invites me to consider how I offer my angel's share. How do I give back to the world a small share of the joy, peace, and goodwill that surrounds me through my faith? How do I return a share of the spirit that angels in our midst have entrusted to me?

The word angel literally means messenger in Greek. This makes sense because that's what angels do: they bring messages from God. The Archangel Gabriel announces to Mary that she will bear God's son, and the Christmas angels praise God and proclaim peace on earth and goodwill to all people. Perhaps we can offer our own angel's share by acting as messengers of peace and goodwill in the lives of all we encounter. Through our actions and interactions, we can bring messages of kindness or compassion, love or friendship. Opportunities to offer our own angel's share abound.

When we pray without ceasing, when we offer compassion, when we lift the lowly, when we work for justice, when we reach out our hands in love to those in need, we offer up our angel's share. When we share our faith with others as an invitation to come and see what gladdens our hearts, we offer up our angel's share. When we allow our hearts to be moved by Jesus's message of peace and love and then act accordingly, we offer up our angel's share.

Cheers, friends.

⇨ ⇨ ⇨

Reflect & Engage

What is your understanding of angels? What tangible ways might you offer your angel's share to the world?

GOLDEN REPAIR

Heal me, O LORD, and I shall be healed; save me, and I shall be saved; for you are my praise. —**Jeremiah 17:14**

Sometime in the fifteenth century, the Japanese Shogun Ashikaga Yoshimasa broke his favorite tea bowl. This wasn't like one of us breaking a wine glass while doing the dishes. For a shogun, a tea bowl had near-mystic qualities. It held a place of prominence in the ancient tea ceremonies of Japan. These gatherings, rooted in ritual and symbol, bound the assembled samurai warriors to their shogun. The tea bowl wasn't just a utilitarian dish; it was a sacred vessel.

Shogun Yoshimasa sent his beloved tea bowl all the way to China to have it repaired. But when it came back months later, he was disappointed. The metal staples used to piece it back together ruined the bowl's character, and it was just... ugly. In desperation, he sent it to a local craftsman whose solution was to fill the cracks with gold.

And thus, a new art form was born. *Kintsugi*, which literally means golden repair, is a method of patching pottery that honors the artifact's unique qualities by emphasizing, rather than hiding, the piece's imperfections. When you see a bowl or a vase that has been repaired this way, the cracks look like a beautiful design feature. The piece takes on an entirely new character even as it retains the original look and shape. And, of course, the alternative is to pitch the broken vessel onto the trash heap.

What I love about this concept is that it views blemishes as beautiful, not shameful. Like human scars that tell stories of courage or survival, these cracks become part of the character and history of the vessel, magnifying its storied journey through ages and empires.

This reminds me of the kingdom of God. It's not a kingdom of power and perfection, but like that broken tea bowl with its golden cracks, it's a reign that embraces humility and vulnerability, blemish, and failure. God's grace fills in the inevitable cracks in our facade and mends the instability of our own foundations.

As with *kintsugi*, our cracks don't magically disappear. Instead, they become part of who we are, part of our identity as beloved, forgiven, and redeemed children of God. The process of being cracked open is often painful and hard. That's the nature of trauma and failure and the surrounding aura of shame. But our cracks often end up becoming avenues to know God in deeper ways. Our brokenness doesn't define us but is an integral part of our story. The cracks help form our beautiful, if imperfect, identities.

As human beings, we are all broken, yes, but through faith in our King of kings and Lord of lords, we are healed and restored and made new in God's very own image.

I think there is great freedom found in the *kintsugi* concept of embracing our flaws rather than hiding them. Imagine all the extra breathing room you'd have if you didn't spend so much energy trying to convince the world everything is okay in your life, especially at moments when it decidedly is not.

We don't need to disguise our cracks. We can value our scars, both visible and invisible, as marks of life and relationship with the living God.

Reflect & Engage

How have you embraced the concept of *kintsugi* in your life over the years? How might doing so empower you in your present circumstances?

PLAYING LIKE BETTY WHITE

Be kind to one another, tender-hearted, forgiving one another, as God in Christ has forgiven you.
—Ephesians 4:32

One of my favorite ad campaigns is the one for Snickers with the tagline, "You're not yourself when you're hungry." You've seen those, right? The most famous one first aired during the Super Bowl in 2010 and featured the late actress Betty White playing football in the mud with a bunch of young men who are obviously frustrated with her lack of athletic skills. When one of her teammates asks why she's "playing like Betty White out there," we realize she's actually the hungry alter ego of a guy named Mike. When Mike's girlfriend runs out and hands over a Snickers bar, Betty White is magically transformed back into Mike, and the game resumes.

I think a lot of us aren't really ourselves these days. We may not be "hangry," the irritability that comes with the hunger candy bars purport to cure, but living through a global pandemic takes its toll. With so many people on edge, it's no wonder so many interactions seem to go sideways.

I know from personal experience that when I'm over-tired or stressed out by things beyond my control, I don't operate as my best self. The graciousness I strive for abandons me, and

I can get a bit cranky in dealing with other people. Most of us are the same way. When we're over-extended or in need of a nap, we tend to get snippy with people.

This is an invitation to all of us, myself included, to be patient with others in the days ahead. The entire world is understaffed and overstressed right now. Since we can't tell by looking at someone's outward appearance what burdens they may be shouldering, our default should be graciousness. In a word, I'm encouraging kindness.

Not everything can be solved by eating a Snickers bar. But when you find yourself "playing like Betty White out there," it's helpful to pause, consider the impact of your actions, and proceed graciously. We could all use some compassion these days, and we could all stand to offer compassion in return.

Reflect & Engage

What are some indications that you're not operating at your highest level? How might you offer more compassion in the world, especially in situations when you don't know what burdens others are facing?

SCIENCE CLASS

Create in me a clean heart, O God, and renew a right spirit within me. —Psalm 51:11

When I was in sixth grade science class, the highlight—or lowlight, depending on your perspective—of the entire year was dissecting a fetal pig. The usually dour Mr. Knipp took great glee in teaching us to slice open the specimens, and he had zero tolerance for squeamishness. I remember one classmate turning green and, on his way to the bathroom, being pelted by a spare eyeball, courtesy of Mr. Knipp. Such was the learning environment at an all-boys prep school in Baltimore in the early 1980s.

What I most remember about the experience, besides the sudden realization that I would never become a doctor, is that the heart was gross. Actually, everything on the inside was gross. But I had high hopes for the heart. The heart is held up as the symbolic life force of every creature. But the heart of my fetal pig wasn't even red. It was just another piece of foul-smelling gray goo. Not exactly the stuff of Valentine's Day cards.

Jesus mentions the heart a fair amount when highlighting the essence of a person's hopes and desires. "Love the Lord your God with all your heart, and with all your soul, and with all your mind," and "Where your heart is, there your treasure will be." When it comes to our spiritual lives, our heart matters; it is the heart of the matter.

Now, if you dig into the Latin, the word for "believe," *credo*, derives from the word *corda*, meaning "heart." This is why to believe in something literally means "to set your heart upon it." Jesus encourages us to set our hearts upon God: to give to God our trust, devotion, and love. This isn't always easy, but doing so (or even attempting to do so) keeps us grounded and connected to God. The heart may have evolved into a long-standing metaphor for our very being, and that's, frankly, where I'd rather keep it. I'm glad there are gifted cardiologists out there, but I prefer to stay in my lane when it comes to matters of the heart: I'll keep encouraging people to give their hearts to God.

The other thing I remember about Mr. Knipp was that he taught his classes while holding a wooden yardstick. If you weren't paying attention, whack! He'd smack that thing on your desk, which was almost enough to make your heart stop.

⇨ ⇨ ⇨

Reflect & Engage

In what ways do you set your heart on God? When you do, how does that impact your interaction with others and with yourself?

CELEBRITY STATUS

I am the LORD *your God, who brought you out of the land of Egypt, out of the house of slavery; you shall have no other gods before me.* —Deuteronomy 5:6-7

A decade ago, I officiated at a wedding for a couple with ties to a major league baseball team. The bride worked for the Red Sox in the publicity department, and the groom produced Red Sox games for the local cable station. In the congregation on their wedding day were a number of former players, including Hall of Famer Jim Rice and pitcher Luis Tiant. Terry Francona was there, even though he had just been fired as the manager. That was the summer after the infamous chicken and beer scandal and the great late-season collapse.

It was a fun day, and they were a great couple. But, in retrospect, I think I was a bit too enamored with the celebrity of it all. I mean, as a kid, I had watched Jim Rice feast on Orioles pitching, smacking home runs over the Green Monster with abandon. I could still mimic Luis Tiant's unique windup from watching him pitch for so many years. And there they were! Sitting in pews!

Now, it's not like I asked for their autograph when they came up for communion. And I played it cool in the post-wedding handshake line. But in the end, no matter who was there, the day was about two people making their vows before God. That's all that mattered. It's not about the reflected glow of being in the presence of celebrity but about being faithful.

Still, we're drawn to the shiny, other-worldly nature of celebrity. It's seductive and intriguing. Recently, I went out to dinner and spotted TV and movie star Steve Carrell sitting at the next table with his family. As a big fan, I demonstrated heroic self-restraint by refraining from asking him for a selfie.

The antidote to celebrity culture is recognizing that we are all children of God and that the object of authentic worship is the one who created us, not the one who graces the cover of *People* magazine. What gives life is the God from whom all blessings flow rather than the celebrities from whom all gossip flows.

It's not wrong to admire people or to cheer for athletes and actors and others who share their talents with the world. It is a good and joyful thing to do just that. But when we find ourselves worshiping our heroes rather than God, we may need a little reality check.

⇨ ⇨ ⇨

Reflect & Engage

When was the last time you encountered a celebrity? How did you act, and how did you feel? In what ways might you transfer hero worship to God worship?

LIFE AND DEATH

He will wipe every tear from their eyes. Death will be no more; mourning and crying and pain will be no more, for the first things have passed away.
—Revelation 21:4

The average American sees a lot of violent images in any given year. Between television, movies, video games, social media, and even the news itself, we are inundated with murder and mayhem. By some counts, the average child will have witnessed 8,000 murders on TV before the end of elementary school. And even if some of those numbers are from watching Wile E. Coyote plummet off a cliff, that's still a lot of death to take in at a very young age.

Think about your TV-watching habits and how many of your favorite shows involve violent crime. From *Murder She Wrote* to *Law & Order*, death sells. I'm not sure why we're so enamored with these kinds of shows or what this says about us.

And it's not as if I'm immune to this grim attraction. I like reading murder mysteries, and among my favorite TV shows is *The Sopranos*. Who doesn't love a good mob hit?

Unfortunately, all this gratuitous violence and death desensitizes us to the real-life suffering in the world. From wars and rumors of wars to hate crimes to political violence, death surrounds us.

Of course, violence has been humanity's constant companion from the beginning of time. All you have to do is pick up your Bible to see the interplay between life and death, peace and war. Jesus himself was violently executed at the hand of the Roman authorities.

The good news in all of this is that God is present with those who suffer. God sides with those who are unjustly persecuted, those who are caught in the crossfire. This means that when we suffer, God is with us as well, loving us, caring for us, tending to us, weeping with us.

I'm not sure why we're so fascinated by plots that involve death. But I take solace in the fact that in the Christian faith, death doesn't get the last word.

Reflect & Engage

Are you drawn to entertainment that includes death? Why do you think that is? Watching or reading through the lens of faith, where do you see God's hand at work?

DOING THE DISHES

But the Lord answered her, "Martha, Martha, you are worried and distracted by many things; there is need of only one thing. Mary has chosen the better part, which will not be taken away from her." —Luke 10:41-42

I am not a great cook. Despite the fact that my mother wrote a cookbook, I didn't inherit her culinary skills. Or interest. Of course, like any good suburban dad, I can barbecue. Obviously. But in the actual kitchen, I am a paragon of mediocrity.

I am, however, an amazing dish washer. Plates, bowls, wine glasses: you use it, I'll happily scrub them clean. My wife, Bryna, complains that I sometimes start washing the dishes before everyone's even done eating. I grudgingly admit that she's right. I don't do it when company's over, usually, but maybe at a random Wednesday night family meal.

The problem with jumping up to do the dishes is that you can miss the point of gathering around the table. It's partly for bodily nourishment, but it's also about building and maintaining relationships. When we focus too much on the mechanics of the meal and its aftermath, the bigger picture gets subsumed by minutiae.

I'm not sure who did the dishes after the Last Supper, but someone must have—such tasks don't just magically happen. But washing these vessels and wiping down the table wasn't just a necessary task. In the context of the Last Supper, it was an act of love on behalf of the gathered disciples. It enabled what really mattered: the relationships.

So often, even with the best intentions, we sacrifice relationships at the altar of getting things done. We focus on the small stuff at the expense of interaction with those who matter most in our lives. The small tasks of life are important, most especially when they allow us to focus on the bigger picture of interpersonal relationships.

Whether it's setting the table or clearing the dishes, these acts are part of the broader context of welcoming, inviting, and connecting with people. When we do that well and with intention, not only is Jesus served, but we become more like him.

I still sometimes focus on the dishes rather than the people around the table. But mostly, I'm able to see this act in the context of what really matters.

⇨ ⇨ ⇨

Reflect & Engage

What tasks in your life do you perform at the risk of ignoring relationships? How do you balance practical tasks that need doing with the importance of focusing on the people in your life?

BACKUP CAMERA

The LORD bless you and keep you; the LORD make his face to shine upon you, and be gracious to you; the LORD lift up his countenance upon you, and give you peace. —**Numbers 6:24-26**

Like most cars these days, my Volkswagen Jetta has a backup camera. At first, I barely used it since my Brooklyn-bred driver's ed instructor beat it into me to actually turn my head and look behind me when moving in reverse. There's still a small part of me that thinks using the backup camera to parallel park is cheating. But I've gotten used to it and have even come to rely on the camera view, especially when navigating the grocery store parking lot.

I recently found myself gazing into it as I was about to transition from one town and parish to another. Pulling out of the driveway for the final time before driving from New England to Florida, I happened to check the camera one more time. And I saw the church I was leaving perfectly framed on a beautiful October afternoon.

Goodbyes are hard. We almost immediately long for the familiar, even amid the excitement of new adventures. Sure, I miss the building where I served God for nearly 14 years, but I miss the people so much more. A quick glimpse into that backup camera brought forth a kaleidoscope of images—faces and laughter, tears and heartbreak. Every single emotion is wrapped up in bidding farewell to the beloved and familiar way things used to be.

I find it important not to dwell on the past, especially on those things that hurt us, but rather to embrace those experiences as a part (but not the whole) of who we are. Our identities are wrapped up in the fullness of our experiences. Even as memories fade and the events of our lives get smaller and smaller in the rearview mirror of life, they remain integral to our lives.

I love the line from the end of Paul's Second Letter to Timothy that reads, "I have fought the good fight, I have finished the race, I have kept the faith" (2 Timothy 4:7). Paul is feeling wistful as he looks back on his life, but he's also looking forward to that time when he will wear the crown of righteousness. He's looking at the backup camera, pausing, and then putting the car into drive and moving forward. That is precisely what we're all invited to do.

⇨ ⇨ ⇨

Reflect & Engage

When was a time you experienced a major transition in your life? What was the hardest part? What brought you joy?

ON THE BENCH

But when you give a banquet, invite the poor, the crippled, the lame, and the blind. And you will be blessed, because they cannot repay you, for you will be repaid at the resurrection of the righteous.
—Luke 14:13-14

When I was in elementary school growing up in Baltimore, there was a bench outside of every classroom. This was not a bench you would use to relax after a hard session of playing dodgeball at recess. This was a different kind of bench: it's where the teacher sent you if you misbehaved.

The threat of being sent to the bench hung over the classroom as a behavioral deterrent. I suppose you were supposed to hang your head in shame as you walked past the other students to sit on the bench and reflect upon the crimes you had committed against both the teacher and all of humanity. But I suspect most kids spent the time praying the principal, Mr. Kirk, wouldn't wander down the hall and drag them into his office for a little chat.

Benches, in general, are tough places. I mean, sure, a judge sits on a bench, and so does an organist, for that matter. But in sports, getting benched is a public acknowledgment that you are underperforming. It is a place of shame, a signal that you don't belong with the real players out on the field. It is a place to fidget and stew and dream about future glory if only you were given a chance. But in the meantime, you chew gum and stare at the action happening inside the lines and beyond your control.

The ancient world also had benches. They weren't outside of classrooms or at sporting arenas, but they stood outside the gates of the homes of the rich. Beggars would congregate on the benches in hopes that the wealthy homeowners would bestow alms upon them. This was a societal norm, part of the social contract. After a great feast, the rich would send leftovers out to those sitting on the bench. The hungry were fed, and the rich felt virtuous in their act of charity.

In one respect, we all take our turn on the bench. We may not be in the situation of those in the ancient world, facing extreme poverty. But we might be in the grips of feelings of grief, unworthiness, guilt, or heartbreak. We may be experiencing physical pain or emotional anxiety or feel overwhelmed by life. There are moments in our lives when we need to sit on the bench and, perhaps even more importantly, ask someone to sit beside us in our pain. It takes vulnerability to ask for help in a culture that idolizes strength. But asking for help and admitting we cannot do it all ourselves is strength in God's vision.

It also takes strength to be the person sitting with those relegated to the benches of life. Imagine if a classmate saw you sitting on the bench and took a seat beside you. They may not be able to save you from impending scholastic judgment, but at least you'd know you weren't alone and that someone was willing to help you face your fears.

We all have seasons of life when we find ourselves sitting alone on the bench. At other times, we find ourselves joining someone on the bench as a sign of support and encouragement. Fortunately, there's no school principal in sight.

Reflect & Engage

Who are the people in your life sitting on the bench right now, those who are marginalized for whatever reason? When have you sat on the bench of life, and who joined you to provide comfort?

THE BIG SORT

There is no longer Jew or Greek, there is no longer slave or free, there is no longer male and female; for all of you are one in Christ Jesus. —**Galatians 3:28**

A few years ago, a book came out with the title, *The Big Sort*. The premise, backed up by lots of data, is that while America is more diverse than ever, the places we live have become increasingly crowded with people who look, think, and vote as we do. There are exceptions, of course, but the statistics highlight how we have self-sorted ourselves into tribal groups. We have built a country that lives in a way-of-life segregation, where we choose neighborhoods, churches, and news shows most in line with our lifestyle and beliefs.

The danger in this segregation is the loss of perspective. We don't just fail to walk a mile in someone else's shoes; we don't even take our shoes *off*. Our worldview narrows, and those with whom we disagree become disembodied "others." We dehumanize the other side to the point of becoming mere caricatures. There is no room for dialogue, which stifles our growth and leads us into digging ever-deepening trenches, keeping company with only those already in our tribes.

Believe me, I like my tribe! It's a non-confrontational place of comfort and safety. When I'm with people who think like me, I don't have to explain myself or offer any context. Everyone gets the inside jokes, they know the lingo, and there's enough shared history and culture that life feels easy. Tribes are good, but they can become insular idols when we start to believe that our way is the only way.

Getting out of our respective comfort zones, as hard as it may be, is critical to emotional and spiritual growth. Yes, this can lead to conflict. Sometimes it comes because we're blinded to certain realities, and sometimes we experience conflict because we hold up a mirror to others.

Fortunately, Jesus is always clear about what matters most: loving others and lifting up the downtrodden. When people's actions subvert these non-negotiables, he stands up and speaks his mind, even when it puts him in precarious positions with the powerful.

We may not always feel empowered to be so bold, but even speaking quietly or haltingly is an important way of putting our faith into action. We love the safety of our tribes: they're comfortable and easy. But stepping beyond them for conversation and perspective and even in loving confrontation forces us to open our hearts in new ways.

When I lived in suburban New York, I enjoyed going to the local farmers' market. Sure, the market had the freshest fruits and vegetables, artisanal baked bread, and other delights. But what I loved most was that it was the single most culturally and racially diverse gathering around. No neighborhood or church brought together so many people of different backgrounds. It was a mix of tribes and opinions, languages and colors. We do well to intentionally, even if only occasionally, leave the comfort of our tribes.

Reflect & Engage

How would you characterize your tribe? Where is it most noticeable in your life? How do you seek to leave your comfort zone and experience greater diversity?

NOW BOARDING

Let another praise you, and not your own mouth
—a stranger, and not your own lips. —**Proverbs 27:2**

If you ever want to feel good about yourself—or bad—fly to California. Or Dallas. Or wherever. Just navigate the TSA lines and get to the gate. Once there, you'll encounter a boarding process that is all about status and rank.

It used to be there was first class, and everyone else was lumped into coach. But now, there are so many categories that it's hard to keep up with them all. There are elite and premier and premier elite customers who all get to board first. And then, the sorting continues with the various boarding zones. Zones one and two aren't bad. But it starts to get a bit dicey after that. And woe to those stuck in zone five, for they must gate check their bags and suffer the ignominy of sitting in the back row near the lavatory, past the smug first-class travelers sipping champagne and the elite and premier and premier elite too.

Jesus says, "For all who exalt themselves will be humbled, and all who humble themselves will be exalted." But if you tried to enact this at the airport, you'd get some odd looks, for sure. Living out Jesus's words would mean trading elite status for zone five. You'd give up your cocktail and extra wide seat for no legroom and lavatory fumes.

Now, I know you're not going to do that. But merely seeing and acknowledging the temptation and allure of higher status is an important step to learning to walk more faithfully in the way of Jesus. And seeking to see the world through God's eyes puts us on the right path.

Most of us have been on both sides of the airline divide. I'm a coach flyer, but every once in a while, I happen to get bumped up to first class. And I have to remind myself that just because the flight attendant gives me a smile and a drink as the other passengers struggle to board doesn't mean I'm better than they are.

I wonder how we might find ways outside the airport to live into Jesus's words. What are some ways we might give away power and status to those who find themselves in the zone five of life? How might we humble ourselves in order to lift up those who are continually trampled upon? We can start by working for justice in the world by amplifying the voices of those whose voices traditionally go unheard. We can share our resources with those who carry substantial economic burdens or debt. We can offer a kind word to anyone who is lonely or sick or fearful. And we can be mindful that we are all created equally in the image of God.

⇨ ⇨ ⇨

Reflect & Engage

What are your impressions and experience with the airline boarding process? How does it inform the way you think about and relate to other people?

ROUND AND ROUND

Therefore thus says the Lord GOD, See, I am laying in Zion a foundation stone, a tested stone, a precious cornerstone, a sure foundation: "One who trusts will not panic." —Isaiah 28:16

Few things make me feel older and sound crankier than when I talk about the playgrounds of my youth. Parents today would never let their children play on them. The metal slides of my childhood scorched exposed skin, and the seesaws threw you off into the nearby dirt or old tire mulch. Like many people my age, I have a small scar on my face from walking too close to the swing set.

My favorite playground equipment was the circular metal apparatus you'd run alongside to make it go as fast as possible before grabbing a metal handle and hopping on. I don't even know what it was called—we referred to it as the whirly gig—but I remember occasionally slipping off and biting the dust, especially if older kids were controlling the speed.

At times, life itself can feel like that ride: exhilarating and slightly out of control with the remote but real possibility that you could get hurt. Life comes fast, with a dizzying array of choices and pitfalls and opportunities. Often, we just want to grab something and hold on for dear life.

We can't always control the speed of life, nor can we ensure that it's a smooth ride. But fortunately, the life of faith offers a tangible guardrail. Spending time with God in prayer is an anchor to keep us grounded, an opportunity to hold fast while the world is spinning.

I'm not suggesting that you sell all your belongings and move into a monastery or convent. I'm talking about simply being connected to God through divine relationship. That might mean saying the Lord's Prayer before bed, offering a short prayer while commuting to work, or saying grace before a meal. This connection to God makes the ride of our lives worth living, even the hard parts, even the moments when we feel as if we're holding on for dear life.

Whatever your prayer practice looks like, when talking with God becomes part of your daily life, no matter how much or how little, it's like having a firm hold on the whirly gig. Whether it speeds up or jerks to a stop, God's got you.

Reflect & Engage

What does your practice of daily prayer look like? What happens when you find yourself out of the prayer habit? How do you draw yourself back into relationship with God?

LOVE YOUR ENEMIES

Do not repay evil for evil or abuse for abuse; but, on the contrary, repay with a blessing. It is for this that you were called—that you might inherit a blessing.
—1 Peter 3:9

Most of us don't have actual enemies. At least not in a dualistic, good vs. evil, Superman vs. Lex Luthor kind of way or even in an antagonistic Road Runner vs. Wile E. Coyote kind of way. But we all have people who annoy us. Boy, do we have people who annoy us. This brings us to what may be Jesus's most difficult teaching: the call to love your enemies.

Even without an avowed archenemy, or at least a neighbor with whom you argue over property lines, it's hard to love those with different viewpoints or perspectives.

We all know people whose beliefs, practices, or worldviews don't align with our own. Some of them show up at our Thanksgiving tables, although many are people we've never met or associated with. We like to lump together "those people" into a nameless, faceless crowd. It's so much easier to tear down people and ideas when we dehumanize them. That's certainly the bread and butter of cable news shows and social media. "Those people" may be out of sight, but they're certainly not out of mind.

This trend toward depersonalization reminds me of road rage: not the extreme version of pulling a gun on a highway but the mild kind that involves cursing under your breath at the clueless driver in the left lane meandering along under the speed limit. Their actions frustrate us, and so we react. But, of course, we don't know what's going on with them personally. The person may simply be a lousy driver, but perhaps they're in the throes of grief or distracted by some difficulty and just trying to make it through the day.

The fact is, we don't know, and Jesus's call to love our enemies is an invitation to humanize one another. What if we approached every interaction with love and compassion rather than suspicion and malice? How might that attitude change the ways we communicate and relate to one another? How might this approach impact our political discourse and our relationships with those with whom we disagree?

If there was a single teaching of Jesus that had the potential to flip the world on its head right now, it would be the call to love your enemies. This call is life-changing, *world-changing*. And it doesn't come with any hedges or caveats. Jesus doesn't say, "Love your enemies unless they post something offensive on Facebook."

We can try to wiggle out of this by insisting we don't have any real "enemies." We're not Luke Skywalker facing down Darth Vader. We're just average people trying to navigate through another day. Still, we can always be more gracious in our interactions with others, especially those who don't see things the way we do. We can work to turn the "other" into a fellow child of God.

⇨ ⇨ ⇨

Reflect & Engage

Have you ever had someone you would consider an enemy, or at least someone you found impossible to interact with? If so, how would you characterize the relationship? In what ways might you approach the situation with more grace and compassion?

BIRTHDAY SONG

For you yourself created my inmost parts; you knit me together in my mother's womb. I will thank you because I am marvelously made. Your works are wonderful, and I know it well. —**Psalm 139:12-13**

Do you get embarrassed when people sing "Happy Birthday" to you? For me, this is one of the most awkward moments in a given year. I know it's coming. All of a sudden, several people disappear into the kitchen, there's a slight hush in the air, and out they come, parading the birthday cake toward me. And then the singing starts. The familiar tune seems to take an eternity, and there's nothing I can do except sit with a goofy smile on my face because, of course, I can't sing "Happy Birthday" to myself.

Don't get me wrong. I appreciate the effort involved, and I love the gathering of family and friends. And I don't mind the presents. It's just that enduring the required serenade while everyone stares at me makes me uncomfortable. And yet, when I'm celebrating someone else's birthday, I'm the first to belt out "Happy Birthday," usually even adding some harmony to the ending. I enjoy making a fuss over someone else much more than I enjoy being fussed over.

It can be hard to let others celebrate our lives. For whatever reason, we often find it difficult to fully accept someone else's love for us. We ask ourselves, "What's the catch?" If someone's going to such great lengths to please me, what am I possibly going to do in return?

This same feeling creeps into the spiritual life when we think about Jesus's love for us. We know intellectually that Jesus loves us: God is love and all that. But when we seek to actualize that love in the deepest recesses of our hearts, we don't always fully believe. Because we know ourselves so well, we think that God cannot possibly love us in all our brokenness, in all our hypocrisy, in all our pride. And yet God still does. God loves us with reckless abandon! Our role is simply to let Jesus have access to our hearts, our thoughts, and our souls—which he does anyway—and then accept his love in our hearts.

I'll never fully be comfortable with people singing "Happy Birthday" to me. But I've come to accept that it's not all about me. And that helps.

⇨ ⇨ ⇨

Reflect & Engage

How do you feel about your birthday celebrations? Do you embrace them, or do they make you slightly uncomfortable? How might you see them as reflections of God's love?

IMAGINE THE POSSIBILITIES

Jesus looked at them and said, "For mortals it is impossible, but for God all things are possible."
—**Matthew 19:26**

We often ask young children, "What do you want to be when you grow up?" And their responses are often shared with great confidence and conviction. Firefighter! Astronaut! President! The answers are full of hope and pregnant with possibility. And why not? At this stage of life, the potential is limitless. Life and limitations haven't gotten in the way, and who knows? Your six-year-old niece may just become a Jedi Master.

This sense of childlike enthusiasm for the future is usually encouraged and embraced by adults. This is partly because we want to empower our children and instill in them the idea that they can do anything or be anything they want to be. And partly, we don't want to rain on their optimism. Reality will eventually set in, but in the meantime, we can wink at their delightful naïvete without crushing their spirit. We want them to dream and explore and have adventures before they settle down and become an accountant.

Just like those kids whose futures are brimming with potential, we may not give our faith a chance to truly grow and blossom. Maybe we let the disappointments and realities of life choke the possibilities. Just when we need it the most, perhaps we stunt our spiritual growth with our rationalism and apathy and failure to see God's hand at work in the world. The hopeful delight that inspires childhood dreams is a precious commodity that, like faith, we don't fully trust.

This doesn't mean all our dreams will come true. That's not how life works. But relationship with God allows us to bear anything thrown our way, as well as to delight in the utter joy of being alive.

Being a pastor was never my childhood fantasy. I always imagined I'd play shortstop for the Baltimore Orioles. Along the way, I grew and matured and realized I didn't have nearly the arm (among other athletic limitations) to make it onto a Major League diamond. Faith, though, was something to delight in. Recognizing that there is more to life than the visible world and that we are loved so fully by our Creator is the stuff that brings wonder to the soul.

Of course, faith isn't some magic formula where if you get the incantation just right, you'll suddenly be able to pull a rabbit out of a hat. Faith isn't fantasy. Nor is it quantifiable. There's no faith-o-meter where, if you reach a certain threshold, you level up. Rather faith is rooted in the intersection of mystery and the hard realities of life. When it comes to faith, hold onto that childhood feeling of possibility.

⇨ ⇨ ⇨

Reflect & Engage

What was your childhood dream? How can you capture a childlike sense of joy and wonder in your spiritual life?

SPIRITUAL WALLFLOWERS

But thanks be to God, who gives us the victory through our Lord Jesus Christ. —**1 Corinthians 15:57**

I used to dread middle school dances. The angst began with the whole, "Should I go or should I just bag it?" Among my circle of friends, conversations went something like this. "You know that dance is on Friday. You going?" "I don't know, maybe. How about you?" "I'm not sure yet. Is Chris going?" "He says he'll go if we go." And so it went until we finally decided we should go—not necessarily because we wanted to but because not going could do more harm to our social reputations.

I usually ended up regretting my decision. There was the awkwardness of it all: the beady eyes of the chaperoning geometry teacher, the loud music that I wasn't really into, the cute girl I secretly liked who someone else had the nerve to ask to dance, and the self-conscious standing around with friends as we tried desperately to look like we were having fun. The technical term for our approach to the whole scene was wallflower.

Sometimes when people think about Christians, they assume we're little more than wallflowers: spiritual doormats who allow ourselves to be trampled upon because we're supposed to be nice. Blessed are the meek and all that.

If you love your enemies, the thinking goes, you'll be exploited. If you do good to those who hate you, you'll be taken advantage of. If you bless those who curse you, you'll become a laughingstock. If you pray for those who abuse you, you'll be bullied. If you turn the other cheek, you'll be smacked again.

Maybe Jesus is soft, a snowflake. We all know that if you really want to succeed in life, you should hate your enemies and do ill to those who hate you and curse those who curse you and abuse those who abuse you. *That's* the recipe for success. Might makes right. Only the strong survive. It's a dog-eat-dog world.

But then we see Jesus triumph over evil, not by stomping his feet and making noise and threatening to rain down fire on his opponents but by loving them, by showing another path, another way to make our way in the world, a way that lifts people up rather than tearing them down.

This approach isn't always easy. Jesus himself is mocked and ridiculed and even put to death. But in the end, love wins out, and freedom reigns. Standing up to the powers and principalities of this world takes great courage and strength. The meek are blessed, not because they are willing to simply lie down and take it but because they are willing to stand up for what they believe in, no matter how countercultural or unpopular. They are powerful because they have aligned their values with God, and nothing demonstrates greater strength than that.

⇨ ⇨ ⇨

Reflect & Engage

In what ways do you live your life at odds with the dominant values of society? How has that impacted the way others perceive you?

CHARACTER ACTORS

I give you a new commandment, that you love one another. Just as I have loved you, you also should love one another. —John 13:34

I've always been intrigued by character actors. They aren't the leading men or leading ladies of the summer blockbuster movie. You'll never see their names on the marquee. You probably wouldn't even recognize them if you bumped into them in the theater lobby while picking up your overpriced and oversized box of Milk Duds.

But character actors are critical to a movie's success, giving the film texture and color. We don't recognize their names, even if they look vaguely familiar in an I-think-he-once-played-a-creepy-killer-on-*Law-&-Order* way.

Beyond their incredible range and ability to inhabit various roles, character actors tend to blend into the background. You don't leave the theater saying, "Wow, the woman who played Tom Cruise's Aunt Suzy was amazing."

Yet, if you read the Bible, really read it deeply and with intention, you start to see some incredible character actors emerge. These are people who aren't necessarily front and center but who play minor, if indispensable, roles in the stories; they are the bystanders, the witnesses, those who stand on the margins of the narrative: the men who lowered the paralytic down through the roof to be healed by Jesus; the parents who brought their children to be blessed by Jesus; the widow who placed two copper coins in the collection plate at the temple.

You can learn a lot from these obscure characters if you choose to notice them. It takes a bit of imagination, but that's half the fun. You begin to wonder, what happened to them? How did their lives turn out following an encounter with Jesus? Some may have dropped everything and followed Jesus. Others undoubtedly returned to their daily lives, touched and transformed by the experience. Still, others may have quickly forgotten the interaction and gone on living as before—fearfully, hopelessly, mindlessly. There are as many reactions to meeting Jesus as there are people who meet him.

We also have character actors in our own lives, people who don't necessarily play a starring role but who are important in the backdrop of our lives. We can ignore them or treat them as minor characters, placed in our path to serve us or simply share the air we breathe. Or we can acknowledge them as fellow children of God, people who play a starring role in their own lives and orbits of friends and family.

We are, of course, all interconnected, and no one is expendable. That's simply how life is set up in the grand scheme of things. Be mindful of the minor actors in your life and give them the respect and dignity they so deserve.

Remember that for others, you may be the minor actor.

⇨ ⇨ ⇨

Reflect & Engage

Who are some of the character actors in your life? How might you treat them in ways that value their intrinsic worth in God's eyes?

JOY TO THE WORLD

So you have pain now; but I will see you again, and your hearts will rejoice, and no one will take your joy from you. —John 16:22

When my brother Matt was in middle school, he took up the trumpet. We were a pretty musical family, at least in theory. Dad was a symphony orchestra conductor, and mom sang in the church choir. My brother and I mostly just started and stopped a bunch of instruments over the years. Between the two of us, we blasted through the violin, piano, French horn, cello, guitar, and the aforementioned trumpet.

What I remember most about Matt's trumpet-playing days is that he could only play one song. It was in the key of C, so it was a fine song for a beginner to learn. The first eight notes were simply a descending scale. But there's only so much "Joy to the World" you can take. Especially in July.

After hearing him play this incessantly and at top volume for weeks, the point came when I'd finally had enough. Now, they make mutes for the trumpet, devices that go into the horn to dampen the sound. If you've ever seen an old video of Dizzy Gillespie, you've seen these things. Matt's rental trumpet came with a mute, but he refused to use it because it made the instrument much harder to play. Well, one day, after hearing "Joy to the World" a hundred times too many, I grabbed the trumpet and shoved that mute so far in that it never came out again. Ever. And that was the end of Matt's trumpet playing career.

The lesson here is not that I was a jerk as an older brother, although I had my moments. Or that hearing the same song over and over again isn't incredibly annoying. It is. Rather, I share this story as a reminder that no matter how hard we try, the joy brought to the world through our faith can never be muted. No matter what darkness we confront, no matter what evil we encounter, and no matter what hardships we endure, the joy of God's love can never be silenced. The joy of the Lord will not be muted.

That's the thing about the life of faith: it doesn't mean that things are always easy for us or without troubles. But in the end, the joy of knowing that you are loved by your Creator is what matters. Joy is our operating system, and nothing can ever delete that or take it away. Jesus is infused in our daily lives if only we open our eyes to the unimagined possibilities of divine relationship. Joy to the world, indeed.

⇨ ⇨ ⇨

Reflect & Engage

When and where have you found joy, even during difficult times of your life? What are some moments when joy has surprised you? How has God shown up in unexpected ways?

ACKNOWLEDGMENTS

As I completed this book, I became rector of the Church of Bethesda-by-the-Sea in Palm Beach, Florida. Times of transition always bring about reflection and introspection, and I'm grateful for a chance to pause and look back on the years of fruitful ministry in the places I've lived and served. Many of the jumping-off points for these devotions have come from family and parish life. And that's been the whole point: to help people see how God moves in the everyday bustle of daily life.

We are inextricably formed by the people we journey with and the experiences we undergo. Thus, any writer is indebted to countless folks who have impacted their lives in myriad ways. I am most grateful for the parishioners at St. John the Evangelist in Hingham, Massachusetts, where I served for nearly 14 years. Many of the experiences in this book took place or were written during my time there.

I'm thankful to the team at Forward Movement, especially Richelle Thompson, who saw potential in my crazy idea to write an unconventional book of devotions.

To Forward Movement Executive Director Scott Gunn, my avowed "archnemesis" and Lent Madness collaborator: I am so glad you're able to keep doing the work you have been given to do. The Church is better for your presence, leadership, and passion for Jesus.

While my wife, Bryna, and I are freshly minted empty nesters, our children, Ben and Zak, never cease to amaze and inspire me. What a joy to watch them become young men and pursue their dreams.

Finally, to Bryna, I couldn't imagine this journey of life and faith without you. You truly are my rock.

ABOUT THE AUTHOR

Tim Schenck serves as rector of the Church of Bethesda-by-the-Sea in Palm Beach, Florida. Creator of the wildly popular online devotion Lent Madness, Tim previously served parishes in Maryland, New York, and Massachusetts. Tim lives in the Bethesda rectory with his wife, Bryna, and two rescue dogs, Cooper and Daisy Duke.

ABOUT FORWARD MOVEMENT

Forward Movement inspires disciples and empowers evangelists. While we produce great resources like this book, Forward Movement is not a publishing company. We are a discipleship ministry. We live out this ministry by creating and publishing books, daily reflections, studies for small groups, and online resources. People around the world read daily devotions through *Forward Day by Day*, which is also available in Spanish (*Adelante día a día*) and Braille, online, as a podcast, and as an app for smartphones.

We actively seek partners across the church and look for ways to provide resources that inspire and challenge. A ministry of the Episcopal Church since 1935, Forward Movement is a nonprofit organization funded by sales of resources and gifts from generous donors.

To learn more about Forward Movement and our work, visit us at forwardmovement.org or venadelante.org. We are delighted to be doing this work and invite your prayers and support.